D1737336

PERSPECTIVES

A Multicultural Portrait of
America's Music

By David P. Press

Marshall Cavendish
New York • London • Toronto

Cover: Rock 'n' roll superstar Tina Turner is joined by Canadian rocker Bryan Adams at a concert to raise money for environmental causes. Turner has excited fans of rock 'n' roll and rhythm and blues for more than two decades. In 1993, her tumultuous life and career became the subject of *What's Love Got to Do With It?*, a popular and critically acclaimed Hollywood movie.

Published by
Marshall Cavendish Corporation
2415 Jerusalem Avenue
P.O. Box 587
North Bellmore, New York 11710, USA

Edited, designed, and produced by Water Buffalo Books, Milwaukee

Project director: Mark Sachner
Art director: Sabine Beaupré
Picture researcher: Diane Laska
Editorial: Valerie Weber
Marshall Cavendish development editor: MaryLee Knowlton
Marshall Cavendish editorial director: Evelyn Fazio

Editorial consultant: Mark S. Guardalabene, Milwaukee Public Schools

Picture Credits: © Archive Photos/American Stock: 41 (bottom); Sabine Beaupré: 68 (top); © The Bettmann Archive: 8, 10, 11 (both), 14 (both), 15, 16 (bottom), 17 (bottom), 18, 19, 20, 21 (both), 22, 24, 26, 27, 29, 30 (both), 31, 32, 33, 34, 35, 36, 37 (both), 38, 39, 40 (both), 41 (top), 42 (both), 43, 46, 48, 51 (all), 52 (both), 53 (both), 54 (both), 56, 57, 58, 60, 61 (both), 63, 64, 65 (all), 66 (both), 67, 68 (bottom), 69 (both), 70 (both), 72 (both), 73 (both), 74 (top), 75; Courtesy of NASA: 23 (bottom); © Reuters/Bettmann Archive: Cover, 6, 16 (top), 17 (top), 23 (top), 44, 71, 74 (bottom)

Library of Congress Cataloging-in-Publication Data

Press, David Paul.
    A multicultural portrait of America's music / David P. Press.
       p.   cm. — (Perspectives)
    Includes bibliographical references and index.
    ISBN 1-85435-687-9 (set). — ISBN 1-85435-666-6 (volume)
    1. Popular music—History and criticism—Juvenile literature. 2. Music and society—Juvenile literature. [Popular music—History and criticism.] I. Title. II. Series: Perspectives (Marshall Cavendish Corporation)
ML3470.P74 1994
781.64'09—dc20

93-48847
CIP
MN AC

To PS – MS

Printed and bound in the U.S.A.

CONTENTS

About *Perspectives*

Perspectives is a series of multicultural portraits of events and topics in U.S. history. Each volume examines these events and topics not only from the perspective of the white European-Americans who make up the majority of the U.S. population, but also from that of the nation's many people of color and other ethnic minorities, such as African-Americans, Asian-Americans, Hispanic-Americans, and American Indians. These people, along with women, have been given little attention in traditional accounts of U.S. history. And yet their impact on historical events has been great.

The terms *American Indian, Hispanic-American, Latino, Anglo-American, Black, African-American*, and *Asian-American*, like *European-American* and *white*, are used by the authors in this series to identify people of various national origins. Labeling people is a serious business, and what we call a group depends on many things. For example, a few decades ago it was considered acceptable to use the words *colored* or *Negro* to label people of African origin. Today, these words are outdated and often a sign of ignorance or outright prejudice. Some even consider *Black* less acceptable than *African-American* because it focuses on a person's skin color rather than national origins. And yet *Black* has many practical uses, especially to describe people whose origins are not only African but Caribbean or Latin American as well.

If we must label people, it's better to be as specific as possible. That is a goal of *Perspectives* — to be as precise and fair as possible in the labeling of people by race, ethnicity, national origin, or other factors, such as gender, sexual orientation, or disability. When necessary and possible, Americans of Mexican origin will be called *Mexican-Americans*. Americans of Irish origin will be called *Irish-Americans*, and so on. The same goes for American Indians: when possible, specific Indians are identified by their tribal names, such as the *Chippewa* or *Mohawk*. But in a discussion of various Indian groups, tribal origins may not always be entirely clear, and so it may be more practical to use *American Indian*, a term that has widespread use among Indians and non-Indians alike.

Even within a group, individuals may disagree over the labels they prefer for their group: *Black* or *African-American? Hispanic* or *Latino? American Indian* or *Native American? White, Anglo*, or *European-American?* Different situations often call for different labels. The labels used in *Perspectives* represent an attempt to be fair, accurate, and perhaps most importantly, to be mindful of what people choose to call *themselves*.

A Note About *America's Music*

At one point in the movie *West Side Story*, members of the Sharks, a Puerto Rican youth gang, whistle an ironic rendition of "My Country 'Tis Of Thee."

The bigotry they experienced, and the history of prejudice and intolerance toward racial minorities and immigrants that it represents, scored the normally simple, patriotic tune with a tinny, hypocritical ring.

The painful paradox is that the United States of America, the greatest social democracy of the modern world, is riddled with a heritage of racism and discrimination and has been stingy at best in extending social freedoms to women. But music, which has always been so much a part of daily life in the U.S., is a paradox within the paradox. There is perhaps no better argument for diversity, no better proof of the benefits of diversity, than a study of America's popular music.

This is not to say there has been no discrimination. The great African-American bandleader Cab Calloway was once arrested for trying to enter a "whites-only" club to hear Lionel Hampton, another African-American musician. Countless songs were stolen from Black R & B artists only to be "cleaned up" and recorded by white singers. Hundreds of Jewish and European ethnic musicians were pressured to change their names to hide their ethnic identities and so gain public acceptance. And throughout U.S. music history, female musicians were not taken seriously unless they were singers. But still, the music industry has often been a pocket within our culture where diversity has flourished, where people of talent, regardless of their race, religion, ethnic stripe, gender, sexual preference, physical abilities or disabilities, have created music and enriched the lives of all their listeners.

From the earliest American folk music to the latest hip-hop, popular music in the United States has been an overlapping succession of types and genres, each different, but each arising from the racial and ethnic corners of American culture. Often, when a new form of music grabs the nation's popular imagination, it soon after becomes commercialized, imitated, and exaggerated. Within a period ranging from a year to ten or more, the music may eventually become a pretty and polished shell of its original form, drained of the vitality and wildness that first made its listeners feel so alive. But then, in more cases than not, the music industry reaches back into America's secret cupboard of creativity — the racial and ethnic neighborhoods, the backwoods communities, the seedy districts of America's cities — to discover the next sensation. And the cycle begins again.

As one form of music after another has become commercially popular, the originals, the people who helped create that music, have rarely gotten their fair share of the financial rewards. But they can still get the credit they deserve. This look at our popular music will celebrate its diversity and recognize that those Americans who have been disdained and discriminated against the most are the very artists to whom we owe the largest debt of gratitude for their legacy of musical creativity.

A young dancer at a powwow in Kamloops, British Columbia. For American Indians, music is not merely entertainment, it is an important part of daily life and cultural identity.

CHAPTER ONE

From Folk Music to World Music

A Sioux Indian reservation in Pine Ridge, South Dakota, 1890. Elsewhere throughout the United States, music is playing. Sentimental ballads and novelty songs are belted out from vaudeville stages in theaters dotting the East Coast, ragtime piano echoes from nightspots along the Mississippi River, Dixieland jazz invents itself in New Orleans, and the blues and bluegrass express the pains and hopes of people in rural communities across the land. But here on the government-managed reservation, several hundred Sioux have gathered for a different kind of music. This isn't ancient tribal music, although it is performed in the ancient, tribal ways. It is a new ceremony of singing and dancing that has spread like a grass fire among the once-mighty tribes of the Plains, from the Paiute to the Arapaho, from the Cheyenne to the Sioux. It is a ceremony that is historical yet visionary, revolutionary yet holy. Indian people call it the Ghost Dance.

Arrayed in beaded buckskins and the splendor of medicine paint and holy feathers, the men, women, and children join hands and dance in a slow circle while singers inside the circle chant. The songs tell of the not-too-distant past, of the glorious days before white men destroyed the great buffalo herds on which the Plains Indians based their economy and their religion. They tell of a time before the people themselves, once so proud and free, were slaughtered by the U.S. Cavalry and herded onto reservations that were little more than prison camps. And the songs tell of the future, of the return of the mighty Indian warriors who drive before them great buffalo herds, ushering in an era of ecological rebirth, peace, and joy. The nervous government agent in charge of the reservation watches the spectacle with a growing sense of alarm.

The Many Folk Musics of America

Because the North American people are made up of many peoples, our music is diverse. The American Indians, the European explorers and settlers, the African slaves, the waves of immigrants from Asia, Europe, and Latin America, and the descendants of each of these groups have contributed their music to make our tradition the richest and most varied in the world. Our

In this Hopi rain ceremony, song, dance, and ritual attire combine to help the people communicate with the spirit world.

oldest music is called folk music, and we enjoy a heritage of folk music reflecting the cultures of people from five continents. The musical traditions of the American Indians, of African-Americans, of Europeans and Latinos, and of Asians not only continue to live today in pure folk forms, but also have influenced blues, country, rock, and nearly all of the popular forms of our national music. Understanding our folk music traditions can help us better appreciate our favorite recording stars of today and their debt to the ethnic musics that began it all.

The Oldest Music in America

The oldest music of our land is in the ceremonial singing of American Indians. But because of the hostility and disrespect that European-Americans have shown for American Indian people and their culture, Native American music has had little influence on our other national musics. In 1500, American Indians numbered three million people living in several hundred tribal communities, each with its own language and songs. By the time of the Ghost Dance in 1890, these three million were reduced through warfare, disease, and starvation to a population of less than a half million. Their culture, traditions, and music were nearly destroyed. Fortunately, the Indian people and their music survived, and Indian culture has been making a slow, difficult comeback throughout the twentieth century.

Traditional Indian life was hung on a string of ceremonies, and each ceremony had its songs and dance. Within this tribal world, songs were not mere entertainments, they were agents of change. Songs could be sung to help a sick person get well, to make crops grow, to carry a dead person's spirit into the afterlife, to bestow bravery and plain good luck on a warrior about to do battle. Music and magic rolled up into one, these tribal songs connected humans with their higher powers in the spirit world.

The traditional Indian song is often a chant or incantation of sounds without words. In other cases, the words tell the story of a successful battle, hunt, or healing. Drums, rattles, flutes, and whistles provide the rhythm and melody, as does the jingling of ornaments on the dancers' costumes. There are almost always dancers, and the movement of their bodies is very much part of the song.

Powwows and Recording Studios.

Today there is both a revival of traditional Indian music and an increasing influence of Indian music on other musical styles. The custom of the powwow, a gathering of many tribes for song, dance,

Singing as a team sport

Not all tribal songs were sacred and serious. A favorite game of the young braves of the Menominee involved hiding objects inside moccasins. Players would divide up into two teams and challenge each other to guess which beans or colored stones were in which moccasin. The skill lay not only in the strategy of hiding and detecting, but also in the craft of singing. Each side would take turns singing songs both to confuse its opponent and to bring luck to itself.

and ceremony, has grown and become an important way to preserve and pass on Indian culture and music. Several professional groups, such as the Ponca Singers and the Sioux Hunkpapa Oka performers, have even become stars of the powwow circuit, much in demand and respected for their ability to perform the traditional songs with skill, flourish, and fidelity to the original spirit. And the American Indian Dance Theater has made a professional stage show of tribal ceremonies that has dazzled audiences in cities across the U.S.

While American Indian cultures have always borrowed songs from other Indian groups and absorbed music from the outside, recently the influence has flowed the other way. As early as the 1920s, there was a brief craze for "Redskin bands," but this was a novelty music that catered to racial stereo-types and not a reflection of a sincere interest in Indian music. Beginning in the 1960s, however, American Indian musicians began quietly to leave their mark on the American music scene. Combining American Indian, African-American, and even Celtic and Saxon folk traditions, Buffy Sainte-Marie, Patrick Sky, and A. Paul Ortega contributed significantly to the folk revival of the 1960s and 1970s. At the same time, the groups Redbone and Xit mixed Indian themes and rhythms with electric rock instruments to create a unique sound. Tom Bee, the leader of the group Xit, whose song lyrics supported the militant American Indian Movement, also worked for Motown, writing and producing records for the Jackson Five. Today his son, Robby Bee, heads up an integrated American Indian/African-American group, Rappers from the Rez. Indian country crooner Neal McCoy has established himself in the traditionally white field of Nashville country, and new age enthusiasts have rediscovered the spiritual quality of traditional Indian music. Carlos Nakai and Douglas Spotted Eagle are Indian flutists making a big splash with folk-influenced, new age albums.

Singing Conquistadors and Latin Folk Music

Picture an adobe mission, a simple Catholic church, in the windblown foothills of New Mexico in 1620. As the service begins, a choir of Zuni Indians raise their voices to sing a Spanish hymn. The first Europeans to settle America were the Spanish, and their first musical footprints were religious songs. As the conquistadors hacked their way from Florida to the West Coast, clearing the way for church settlements, their *padres* soon found that music and musical instruments were great aids in selling Christianity to the Indians. But Spanish settlers soon concentrated on Mexico and the Caribbean, and Hispanic music did not make itself heard in the U.S. until after it worked its way back here through Mexico, Cuba, and Puerto Rico. By then, it was so colored by Indian and African traditions that it is hardly recognizable as European anymore.

Once within the culture of Mexico, the Spanish folk romance became the *corrido*. While the romance was a song about the adventures of medieval knights, *corridos* mixed a little journalism with history and folk mythology. Throughout the nineteenth century, it was the *corrido* that recounted in song the Indian uprisings and battles for Mexican independence. These folk

Grammy award-winner Linda Ronstadt, just one of many Mexican-Americans who have helped shape recent music.

ballads, often going on for two dozen or more stanzas, have survived into modern-day Mexican-American communities. Modern *corridos* have told the legends of Cesar Chavez and Martin Luther King, Jr., while others tell the stories of brave individuals who stand up and fight a corrupt and cruel establishment, usually the Texas Rangers.

Today, in South Texas and in rural communities all along the migrant-worker circuit, Mexican-American folk music thrives. Variously known as Tex-Mex, *Tejano*, or *norteno*, this music features songs about romance, violence, and outlaws. Played by *conjuntos*, four- or five-piece bands led, of all things, by hot-blooded accordion players, *Tejano* features rollicking dance music that mixes traditional Mexican folk, electric rock, and German polka. The best-known *conjunto* today is the Grammy-winning group The Texas Tornadoes. Led by *accordeonista* Flaco Jimenez, The Tornadoes also feature Freddie Fender and Doug Sahm. In the 1960s, Sahm headed a Tex-Mex group called the Sir Douglas Quintet that posed as Beatles imitators complete with British accents, and in the 1970s Fender successfully crossed over into country and western stardom with such hits as "Wasted Days and Wasted Nights."

Many other Mexican-American musicians have successfully mastered a variety of American musical styles. Ritchie Valens, one of the original rockers from the 1950s, had a huge hit with a rock version of "La Bamba," a Mexican folk song. Thirty years later, "La Bamba" was again a smash hit, this time recorded as a tribute to Valens by the group Los Lobos. Singer Linda Ronstadt moved with equal skill from rock to country to pop love songs before returning to her Mexican roots to record Mexican ballads. Blues guitarist Tino Gonzales brings a distinctly Mexican influence to his unique style of Latin rhythm and blues. And one of the hottest 1990s rap groups is Cypress Hill, fronted by Los Angeles-area Mexican-Americans B-Real (Louis Freese) and Sen-Dog (Senen Reyes).

Folk Music from the Caribbean

Hispanic Influences. Cuba, Puerto Rico, the Dominican Republic, and Central and South America have also been rich sources of Hispanic folk music in the United States. The folk music of the *Indios* of the Andes Mountains and of Central America features Spanish lyrics accompanied by native instruments such as rainsticks, panpipes, flutes, and bongo-style drums. Folk-rock star Paul Simon has helped popularize this music in the United States, and such traditional tunes as "El Condor Pasa" and "Moliendo Cafe" have influenced the growing styles of new age and world music.

Many popular dances of the twentieth century, including the cha-cha, the rhumba, mambo, and samba, are direct imports from the folk musics of Cuba and Puerto Rico. As Spanish slave traders of the seventeenth and eighteenth centuries brought Africans to the Caribbean nations they conquered, the folk music that developed showed a strong African influence. Set apart from other North American Hispanic music, this Afro-Caribbean music with its complex rhythms has had a major impact on North American jazz and rock. Today, Cuban-American singer Gloria Estefan proudly shows off the influence of her Caribbean roots in her music, particularly in her beautiful and daring all-Spanish album, *Mi Tierra*.

Steel Drums and Other Caribbean Musics. The music from Jamaica, the British West Indies, and Haiti differs from the Hispanic music of the Caribbean but also has left its influence on music of the U.S. From Trinidad and Jamaica comes folk music with African and British coloring. Traditionally, the island musicians played steel drums, fashioned from empty oil barrels, and homemade clarinets. Their simple love songs and humorous ballads known as mento and calypso music became popular in the U.S. in the 1950s. Ella Fitzgerald had a big hit with "Stone Cold Dead in the Market," but Harry Belafonte became the king of American calypso with such classics as "Day-O" and "Jamaica Farewell." More recently, reggae and ska have had a major impact on rock. With its English lyrics, Caribbean rhythms, and themes of social justice, reggae became significant in the 1970s. Not only did reggae influence music and musicians outside of the Caribbean, but Jamaican originals such as Bob Marley and Jimmy Cliff became U.S. and international stars. Ska, a version of reggae that incorporates trumpets, saxophones, and jazz band arrangements, is practiced by many rock groups such as Britain's UB40. Together with reggae and soca (Caribbean disco music), ska is contributing to the growing popularity of world music.

Top: Cuban-American singer Gloria Estefan has had huge hits with both English- and Spanish-language albums.
Bottom: Twenty-five years before reggae, calypso singer Harry Belafonte popularized Jamaican music in the United States.

Haitians and French-Canadians Harmonize in New Orleans

For a brief period in the early eighteenth century, France flexed its muscles, reached across the Atlantic, and set up colonies in Canada, the Mississippi Delta region of Louisiana, and Haiti and Martinique in the Caribbean. But by 1755, when British troops rounded up thousands of French-Canadians, burned their homes, and forced their exile from the Acadia region of Canada, France had lost most of its political influence in the Americas. Fortunately for us today, French music was more resilient. From France, from Canada, and from the Caribbean, three strains of French music converged in Louisiana to produce the Cajun and zydeco folk musics that are among the most popular in the United States.

Many of the French-speaking refugees from Canada resettled in the rural bayous of Louisiana. There, nearly isolated from the rest of the world until oil was discovered in the swamps in the 1930s, the people from Acadia became known as "Cajuns," and they played music to keep their past alive. Sung in the Cajun dialect, a folk language of French spiced with some Indian, Spanish,

"Son of a gun, gonna have big fun on the bayou."

The invasion of Louisiana by the oil industry also launched a tradition of "pop" Cajun songs that abandoned Cajun dialect for English and added guitars and drums to the traditional instruments of fiddle, accordion, and steel triangle. This Cajun offshoot includes many great songs and recording artists, including the classics "Jambalaya," by Hank Williams, and "The Battle of New Orleans," by Johnny Horton. Dr. John, Doug Kershaw, Credence Clearwater Revival, and Emmy Lou Harris are other singers who have cracked the country and rock charts with Cajun-inspired hits.

German, and African expressions, the songs told of the loneliness, sorrow, and lost loves that were the aftermath of the Cajun people's forced exile from Canada, known as *Le Grand Derangement*.

Several times this century, Cajun culture and music have rebounded from the brink of extinction. In an act of attempted cultural assassination, the Louisiana government outlawed the Cajun language from the schools in 1916, forcing a generation of Cajun children to learn English only — a language their parents could not speak. Then, after Cajun country was opened to the rest of America by the oil industry in the 1930s, many younger Cajuns saw the old songs as old-fashioned "chank-a-chank" music. Country swing became the new dance music in the area, and only the old-timers preserved the tradition.

But the traditional Holler style of Cajun songs was kept alive in the 1950s by the blind accordionist Iry LeJeune. When LeJeune died in 1955 at the age of twenty-six, however, few people outside of Cajun country took notice. Then, at the Newport Folk Festival in 1964, Dewey Balfa, the fiddle-playing son of a sharecropper, became the find of the festival when he sang simple Cajun ballads and brought the audience of fifteen thousand to a frenzy. Since then, Michael Doucet and his Grammy-winning group Beausoleil have continued the Cajun revival. But even though the music has been "discovered" in the U.S., Canada, and France, only a select few Cajun musicians can claim to support themselves by their music.

Zydeco: Black Creoles and Green Bean Music

A particularly flashy version of Cajun music that was developed by African-American musicians from the region is known as zydeco. Taking its name from the Cajun word for green beans (les haricots, pronounced "lay zydeco"), zydeco music has roots that go back to the wild folk dances of Louisiana plantation slaves before the Civil War. The French-speaking plantation owners in Louisiana were known as Creoles. Directly descended from France, the Creoles distanced themselves from the Cajuns and considered themselves the upper class of Louisiana. The Creoles imported their slaves from West Africa, often bringing them first to Haiti. Along the way, these Africans learned to speak French, or at least their own version of it, and became known as Black Creoles.

Beginning in 1817, slaves from area plantations were allowed on Sundays to meet at a New Orleans plaza called Congo Square. There, often before large crowds of white spectators, participants would drum and dance and sing in an effort to piece back together the musical ceremonies of West Africa. This "voodoo music" eventually influenced and took from jazz, the blues, and even early rock 'n' roll to form zydeco. Accordion legend Amedee Ardoin pioneered modern zydeco in the 1930s, and in the 1950s, Boozoo Chavis and Clifton Chenier became role models for the zydeco artists of today. As practiced by Stanley Dural (better known as Buckwheat Zydeco), Rockin' Dopsie, Dopsie Junior, and others, contemporary zydeco differs from traditional Cajun by eliminating the fiddles and using a saxophone or trumpet, cowbells, and an instrument known as a *frottoir*, a modified laundry washboard worn as a vest.

Folk Music: A Powerful Presence

The Tradition from Britain and Ireland. Until recently, most music historians used the term "folk music" to refer mostly if not exclusively to the ballads, love songs, and fiddle tunes that came to us from England, Scotland, and Ireland. Although we now know that this Anglo-Celtic tradition is only one stream of the many folk musics of our culture, it is still a rich one that inspired bluegrass, country, and, in part, rock 'n' roll. For centuries, these original folk songs changed very little as they were handed down from parent to child in the true oral tradition. The ballads were simple songs, condensed, dramatic stories with a tune that helped to set the mood. But there were also love songs such as "Black Is the Color of My True Love's Hair" and game songs such as "Skip to My Lou." They were always sung from memory, sometimes unaccompanied by instruments. But when instruments were used, they were usually the dulcimer, banjo, guitar, and fiddle. Irish jigs, Scottish reels, and other fast dance tunes often had no lyrics.

Folk Music and the Depression. The years 1929 to 1931 were the beginning of a long nightmare for most Americans. Thirty thousand businesses folded, ten million people lost their jobs, and twenty-five hundred banks closed. Everyone who had money deposited in those banks lost it. There was no such thing as food stamps, unemployment checks, or depositors' insurance. For millions of Americans, feeding their families became a daily battle. Many lost.

In the face of such mass poverty and hardships, a large community of American artists, intellectuals, and people of good will emerged to support workers and the oppressed in their fight for better living conditions and social change. Much to the astonishment of the rural families who had preserved these songs for generations, folk music became the music of choice of America's political activists. It was the people's music, and the songs became anthems for justice.

That's how Aunt Molly Jackson became a favorite of the New York coffeehouse set in the 1930s. A midwife, medic, union organizer, and singer for the coal miners in Kentucky, Jackson lost her father, husband, and son to mining accidents. Using traditional rural folk tunes, Aunt Molly would write new lyrics and sing songs at rallies to urge miners to organize for better working conditions. When she was run out of Kentucky in 1931, she resettled in the Greenwich Village neighborhood of New York City, where she continued to write pro-labor, anti-management songs until her death in 1960.

Above: Believing music could change society, Woody Guthrie wrote thousands of simple folk songs with humorous and vivid lyrics in the 1930s and 1940s.

Below: The rebels of the 1960s often heard their passions expressed in the folk-based songs of Bob Dylan and Joan Baez.

But no one epitomizes the folk troubadour of the 1930s more than Woody Guthrie. This singer and vagabond from Oklahoma wrote literally thousands of songs including "Union Maid" and "This Land Is Your Land." Listening to Guthrie's songs is like visiting a museum of America in the 1930s and 1940s. He wrote about the Depression and the dust bowl, about injustice and freedom, about migrant workers and outlaws. And he also wrote dozens of children's songs that have become classics, such as "If You're Happy and You Know It" and "Take You Riding in My Car-Car." Woodrow Wilson Guthrie died of Huntington's chorea, a rare nerve disorder, in 1967, but not before influencing the folk generation of the 1960s.

Vietnam, Civil Rights, and Folk Music. Urban folk music was kept alive in the beatnik coffeehouses of the 1950s, and occasionally a song such as Pete Seeger's "Where Have All the Flowers Gone?" or the Kingston Trio's "Tom Dooley" would crack the Hit Parade. But the decade of the 1960s saw an entire generation turn to folk music to express its anger, its sadness, and its rebellion against the "establishment." Millions of young Americans banded together to oppose the war in Vietnam, to demand equal rights for people of color, and to try out an alternative "hippie" life style that rejected traditional middle-class values. Everywhere they rallied, whether in the nation's capital to march for civil rights, the streets of Chicago to protest the war, or a farm in upstate New York to celebrate three days of peace and love, the citizens of the "counterculture" were accompanied by music, much of it folk and folk influenced.

Led by Bob Dylan and Joan Baez, this new generation of folksingers first came to public attention on the stage of the Newport Folk Festival, an annual event that began in 1959 and by the end of the sixties drew crowds of eighty thousand. From Canada came Leonard Cohen ("Suzanne"), Joni Mitchell ("Big Yellow Taxi"), and Cree Indian Buffy Sainte-Marie ("Universal Soldier"). They joined U.S. balladeers Judy Collins ("Both Sides Now"), Phil Ochs ("I Ain't Marchin' Anymore"), Janis Ian ("Society's Child"), Paul Simon ("The Sound of Silence"), Woody's son, Arlo Guthrie ("Alice's Restaurant"), and others in recording song after song that attacked the values and practices of the establishment and flaunted the values of the counterculture.

From Folk to Folk-Rock. Like Baez and Dylan, the folksingers of the 1960s began where the troubadours of the 1930s left off, by singing traditional Anglo-Celtic ballads and adapting them to the new protest movement. But by mid-decade, Bob Dylan, whose songs had become increasingly original and offbeat, picked up an electric guitar and changed the direction of folk to folk-rock.

A strong, politically outspoken woman, Joan Baez was from the start a crusader with a guitar and a voice of gold.

Nearly every one of her concerts in the 1960s benefited a cause. She sang for migrant farm workers and for civil rights organizations, for the Draft Resistance League and for other peace organizations. She always donated most of the proceeds, living modestly despite her star status. When the American Broadcasting Company (ABC) tried to cash in on the folk movement with a weekly sing-along show, "Hootenanny," Baez boycotted the show because the producers refused to allow longtime political activist Pete Seeger to appear. With the decline of the folk movement in the 1970s, Baez switched to more personal and emotional songs with lush orchestrations, but she has remained a heroine and role model for the folk revival of the 1990s.

Far from the intimate coffeehouses, the Woodstock festival brought half a million young Americans together to listen to many folkies and folk-inspired rockers.

Born Robert Zimmerman into a Jewish family in rural Minnesota, Bob Dylan was to his generation what Woody Guthrie was to the Depression. He began with traditional Anglo folk-ballad forms spiced with sharp-edged lyrics. His songs, such as "Masters of War" and "The Lonesome Death of Hattie Carroll," attacked oppression and defended the underdogs. Other songs, such as "A Hard Rain's A-Gonna Fall" and "The Times They Are A-Changin'," were more poetic and prophetic, warning of doomsday and predicting revolutionary changes on the horizon. "Blowin' in the Wind" became an anthem for all those who believed their generation was riding a tide of change, and it was covered (recorded in different versions) by over sixty artists, including Peter, Paul, and Mary, Duke Ellington, and even aging European film vamp Marlene Dietrich. Forever changing, Dylan moved from folk to folk-rock to country to gospel, often disappointing and losing many fans in the process, but always bringing originality to his efforts. Recently, after nine gold albums and forty albums in all, Dylan has returned to the simpler acoustic folk ballads of his youth.

The Third Wave of Folk. In the 1990s, folk music has shown signs of regaining some of the vitality and popularity it had lost since the 1960s. It is seen in the popular "unplugged" acoustic sessions sponsored by MTV, and it has influenced many alternative groups, including REM, Cowboy Junkies, Indigo Girls, the rap group Arrested Development, and Tempest, a five-piece Celtic folk-rock band led by Norwegian-American Lief Sorbye. But the strongest evidence for a revival is the appearance of a group of young, talented soloists who, with guitars in hand, are bringing audiences back to the coffeehouses and folk festivals.

Nanci Griffith has recorded songs by Woody Guthrie and Bob Dylan as well as her own folk compositions. Tish Hinojosa, who sometimes records Spanish lyrics, is another who gets occasional radio airplay and has helped to popularize folk. Together with Tracy Chapman, Iris Dement, Suzy Bogguss, Michelle Shocked, and Mary-Chapin Carpenter, they form a core of talented

Top: Tracy Chapman, one of the many talented singers leading a folk revival in the 1990s.
Bottom: The "Singing Brakeman," Jimmie Rodgers, generally regarded as the father of country music.

women performers who bend country and blues into folk and keep the heritage of Aunt Molly Jackson and Joan Baez alive.

Country Music and Its Kin

From Hillbilly to Country. The Anglo-Celtic folk tradition also gave rise to country music and to its offshoots, western swing and rockabilly. When America's music industry in the 1920s "discovered" the songs and musicians of rural southern communities, they called it "hillbilly music." They promoted it as novelty music and figured its popularity would soon pass. Little did they realize that country music would become after rock 'n' roll the second-most popular form of music in the U.S.

In 1922, Atlanta radio station WSB led scores of other small stations in broadcasting country music by local performers. The next year, a Georgia moonshiner and fiddler named John Carson made the first country music record, "The Little Old Log Cabin in the Lane" and "The Old Hen Cackled and the Rooster's Going Home." Like most country music before and since, Carson's songs feature high-pitched, nasal singing, lyrics that focus on family, love, death, and religion, stringed-instrument accompaniment, and simple, sincere emotions straight from the gut. So successful was Carson's record that recording industry executives were soon scouring the rural South, portable recording equipment in hand, searching for new stars to discover.

It was on just such a talent search to Bristol, Tennessee, in 1927 that both Jimmie Rodgers and the Carter Family were first recorded and the two main traditions of country music were set in motion. Rodgers sang about the loner, the rambler, the man who had to leave. The Carters sang about mother, God, and the family that had to stay behind. Nicknamed the "Singing Brakeman" because he had worked on the railroad and sang a lot of railroad songs, Rodgers recorded 111 songs and sold twenty million records in the six years between his first record and his death from tuberculosis. And he yodeled. Somewhere in the course of his youthful travels, he picked up this Swiss singing technique and made it a trademark of his songs. With such hits as "T For Texas" and "Any Old Time," Rodgers went on to be a major influence on the next generation of country singers, including Hank Williams, Ernest Tubb, Tex Ritter, and Johnny Cash. Later, Bill Haley, Roy Orbison, Elvis Presley, and other early rockabilly stars of the 1950s were also influenced by Rodgers's music.

The Talented Women of Country Music. From Mother Maybelle Carter to Kelly Willis, K. T. Oslin, and Wynona Judd, country music has led the way in providing opportunities for women artists. Other forms of American music have been all too slow to give women the freedom to compose, sing, and play an instrument. Sara and Maybelle were among the original four members of the Carter Family. Soon joined by three daughters, the group went on to record over 250 songs, including "I'm Thinking Tonight of My Blue Eyes" and "Wildwood Flower," and to set standards of country music for generations of followers. As women's political struggles in the U.S. switched from the right to vote to equal rights in the workplace and freedom from sexual stereotypes, Kitty Wells, Patsy Cline, and Loretta Lynn were but a few of the guitar-picking singer-composers who rose to the top of their field. But while serving as role models for women performers of the seventies, eighties, and nineties, the lyrics of their hit songs, such as Tammy Wynette's "Stand By Your Man," were unfazed by the growing tide of feminism. They led more by personal example than by musical statement.

But in the 1970s, artists Bonnie Raitt, Reba McIntyre, and Emmy Lou Harris emerged as country singers with a conscience, and their innovative songs combined country rhythms with lyrics that touched on personal and political struggle. Mixing rhinestones and country glitter with tremendous individual talent, no one combined traditional country with feminist achievement more successfully than Dolly Parton as she emerged from the shadowy role of Porter Waggoner's lovely assistant to become the "nine to five" superstar. Today, in both mainstream and alternative country, the best songs are being composed and sung by women. Mary-Chapin Carpenter's feminist tune, "Girls With Guitars," became a hit for Wynona Judd, and even sixties folkie Janis Ian has made a comeback with her country tunes that subtly champion feminism and gay rights.

Breaking the Color Line in Country Music. But if the country music industry has been friendly to women artists, until recently it has been a fairly exclusive white, Anglo-Saxon, Protestant domain. Even though the songs of Jimmie Rodgers had a lot in common with the music of African-American blues pioneer Huddie Ledbetter and the Carter Family was influenced by Negro spirituals, country music has remained a white, Christian folk form. Ryman Auditorium, which has served as home for the Grand Ole Opry radio broadcasts since 1925, opened in 1892 as a Pentecostal revival hall. When Kinky Friedman, a Texas musician known for his satirical, tongue-in-cheek country songs, appeared at the Grand Ole Opry in the 1980s, he was uncomfortably introduced as "the first real live Jew to appear on this stage." Recently, however, with American Indian country singer Neal McCoy, Jewish-American songwriter Janis Ian, and the integrated bluegrass-blues duet "Hillbilly Voodoo," the lines between country and other folk musics have begun to blur.

This social and artistic integration began with Charlie Pride, the first African-American country music star. The son of a sharecropper, Charlie Pride played baseball for the Birmingham Black Barons, the same team Willie

Bonnie Raitt (top) and Reba McEntire (bottom) are but two of the many female singer-composer-musicians to rise to the top of country music.

Although country music showed African-American influences from the beginning, Charlie Pride was the first African-American performer to achieve fame as a country music singer.

Mays got his start with, in the final years of the Negro American League before turning his talents to singing.

When he first performed in Nashville in the late sixties, audiences greeted him with expressions of shock, then silence, and eventually polite applause. Within a few years, however, his albums were going gold, and singles such as "Kiss an Angel Good Morning" rose to the top of the country charts. Pride won honor after honor, including a dozen Grammys, leading male vocalist, and country music entertainer of the year. As he achieved superstar status, he won the hearts of country music fans and made it possible for other African-American artists such as Ray Charles and Cleve Francis to record country music albums.

African-American Folk Music

The Africans who were brought against their will to serve as slaves in the American colonies already had a folk music — the tribal, ceremonial songs they brought with them from Africa. During the 250-year course of slavery in the U.S., this music of pulsing and complex drum rhythms proved impossible to preserve completely. Once within the plantation, the folk music of the slaves merged with European traditions and evolved into two strands: communal, religious singing known as spirituals; and solitary songs known as the blues.

Although they became increasingly polished and professional, African-American spirituals survived in post-slavery America with little change until eventually they were influenced by rhythm and blues to form gospel. The folk blues thrived as a rural tradition, then in the 1920s combined with jazz bands to make "city" or "classic" blues, and later, in the 1950s, blues musicians adapted their music to the electric guitar and developed a style called "Chicago" blues.

Let My People Go. When slaveowners tried to teach Protestant church hymns to their slaves, some interesting things happened. They learned the hymns all right. But in both singing style and purpose they gave the songs an interpretation never intended or imagined by the slaveowners.

In plantation after plantation, as the slaves learned the hymns, they sang them in the manner of African tribal folk songs and transformed them into spirituals. Sung without musical instruments, songs such as "Michael Row the Boat Ashore" and "He's Got the Whole World in His Hands" were characterized by intricate vocal harmonies and spur-of-the-moment variations. Rhythmic clapping, swaying, and dancing are other trademarks of the African-American spiritual.

Although the slaveowners of the U.S. wanted to believe that their slaves were simple, happy folk, the fear of slave uprisings was never far from their hearts. The owners hoped that the hymns might pacify the slaves by teaching them about the rewards of the afterlife and urging them to accept their fate on earth. But throughout the seventeenth and eighteenth centuries, slaves whose names we no longer know composed spirituals that were really coded messages. Drawing upon an intimate knowledge of the phrases and images of the Bible, a song such as "Go Down, Moses" is both a religious hymn and a song in code about overrunning the plantation owners and escaping from slavery. Slave owners were delighted with all this singing about Israel, Egypt, and the promised land, until they eventually got the point and realized that Israel stood for the slaves, Egypt for the slave owners, and the promised land for freedom. Proud of themselves for having cracked the code, even if it did take them two hundred years, slaveowners then proceeded to crack down on spiritual-singing slaves. In South Carolina in 1862, an entire congregation of African-Americans was jailed for singing "We'll Soon Be Free," a song about much more than freedom from the bonds of mortal life in heaven.

The Jubilee Singers and Sweet Honey in the Rock. The first professional spiritual choruses appeared soon after the Civil War. When Fisk University, the all-Black college founded in 1866 to educate freed slaves, found itself underfunded and in financial trouble, music instructor George White organized some students into the Jubilee Singers. Presenting a program of spirituals, the group toured the U.S. to raise money for the university.

When the Jubilee Singers appeared at Henry Ward Beecher's renowned Plymouth Church in Brooklyn, the *New York Herald* ran the headline, "Full Troupe of Real Live Darkies in the Tabernacle of the Lord." Despite this kind of press, the group went on to a successful tour of New England, Washington, D.C., and Europe, raising $150,000 for their cause.

In the first half of the twentieth century, African-Americans Paul Robeson and Marian Anderson achieved fame as singers of spirituals. Each sang with operatic skill and great emotion. Today, six African-American women, five singers, and one sign-language interpreter continue and update the tradition. Known as Sweet Honey in the Rock, they tour college campuses with a program of songs sung a cappella (without musical accompaniment) that celebrate the human spirit overcoming oppression.

Marian Anderson: of thee we sing

In 1939, as southern senators filibustered for six weeks to block the passage of an anti-lynching bill, First Lady Eleanor Roosevelt invited African-American opera singer Marian Anderson to give a recital at Constitution Hall. Lynching and mutilation of African-Americans had been an all-too-common practice throughout many southern states since the Civil War, with ten to forty cases reported each year. Even though public outrage seethed at this racist barbarism, U.S. senators incredibly refused to make lynching a federal offense for fear of offending racist white voters in their states. So it only added insult to injury when the Daughters of the American Revolution, the women's group that managed Constitution Hall and of which Mrs. Roosevelt was a member, refused to let Marian Anderson sing, declaring that no Negroes were allowed in Constitution Hall. The First Lady counterpunched hard. She resigned from the D.A.R. and went to the secretary of the interior, Harold Ickes, demanding his permission to use the Lincoln Memorial for a concert.

On a crisp autumn day, twenty thousand Americans, Black and white in equal numbers, mostly families, assembled on the mall. Everyone knew Marian Anderson possessed a rich contralto voice that won her critical acclaim and wild popularity throughout Europe. Everyone knew she was barred from singing in U.S. opera houses because she was Black. And everyone felt the national disgrace of racism that her treatment represented. But on that day, as she began to sing, the proud gathering dressed in their Sunday best were wrapped in the chilling faith and hope of her voice as she rang out the words of her first selection, "America": "From every mountainside, let freedom ring."

Got the Blues So Bad

Rarely has music been as important to human survival as it was to African-American slaves. Spirituals brought people together to express a vision of a better life and a common hope for freedom. Without such sustenance, far fewer would have survived the overwork and undernourishment of slave life. Besides the spiritual, a lonelier, more anguished form of African-American folk song also has its roots in the horrors of slavery. Unlike the group-based spirituals, the "holler" was a simple, hauntingly personal expression of grief in song. A typical holler consists of a few simple sentences punctuated by wails and howls, usually sung while working in the fields or resting in the evening shade. After abolition, these hollers developed into the blues and would eventually influence the singing style of early rock 'n' rollers in the 1950s.

Although the abolition of slavery was a great step forward, it did not signal the end of oppression for African-Americans. Slavery was over, but bigotry and racial prejudice actually became uglier and louder as African-Americans became more visible in day-to-day life. By the turn of the century, professional sports were racially segregated, segregation laws were common throughout the South, and hate groups such as the Ku Klux Klan had gained control of many southern communities. For many former slaves and their children, the Civil War replaced the bondage of the plantation with poverty, isolation, and the threat of violence, and the price of freedom was the feeling of being overwhelmed by a new set of rules. These conditions gave rise to a whole class of wandering bluesmen who sang about work and unemployment, about gambling and drinking, about being stuck in prison and the need to move on. And they sang songs about loss, about lost community and lost love, about the pain of a broken heart. For reasons not entirely clear, many of these folk-bluesmen, such as Lemon Jefferson and Willie McTell, were blind. Nearly all were outcasts from both Black and white society. Forced to live the life of vagrants, they lived as they sang and sang as they lived, often spending time in jail.

"Leadbelly," composer of "Midnight Special" and other classics, was one of the first folk-blues singers to be recorded.

Leadbelly and Country Blues. Nothing captures the spirit of African-American folk-blues better than the life and music of Huddie "Leadbelly" Ledbetter. Part poet and part hoodlum, Leadbelly was twice convicted of homicide and was serving a thirty-year sentence in the brutal Louisiana State Penitentiary when he was discovered by folklorist John Lomax in 1934. Lomax won him a parole and then introduced Leadbelly to the music world. By then his repertoire ranged from songs about the cotton fields of his youth, such as "The Boll Weevil" and "Pick a Bale of Cotton," to "See See Rider" and other country blues he composed while rambling around Texas and Louisiana, to chain-gang and prison songs such as "Midnight Special." Like other country- and folk-blues artists, Leadbelly accompanied himself on guitar and harmonica. His sharp, colorful lyrics drew vivid pictures and used rhyme in ways that went far beyond the moon-June-spoon techniques of conventional songwriters.

W. C. Handy and Classic Blues. From 1920, when Mamie Smith had a hit record with the first blues record, "You Can't Keep a Good Man Down," through the mid-1930s, a jazzed-up form of blues now known as "classic blues" enjoyed a huge popularity and commercial success. Unlike country blues, classic blues almost always featured a woman singer, sometimes accompanied by just a piano, other times backed by some of the best jazz combos around. The songs, some of the most lusty and sexually explicit ever recorded, were usually about love, jealousy, and betrayal. Memphis Minnie, Victoria Spivey, Ma Rainey, and Bessie Smith defined this music, but it was William "W. C." Handy who imported country blues into the world of the big city.

W. C. Handy, song-writer who first composed jazz-band versions of country-blues melodies.

Handy was an aspiring band leader, composer, and music publisher in 1903 when he found himself late one night at a railway station, waiting for a train, listening to a ragged, blind musician slapping a homemade guitar and wailing a song about lonesome traveling. Rapt, Handy put a dime in the musician's cup from time to time to keep him playing like a human jukebox. Although he is often called "the father of the blues," Handy was really the transcriber of the blues, and as he listened, he feverishly wrote down the notes he heard. With great skill, Handy later converted these notes and chord progressions into dozens of blues songs orchestrated for bands and so built the bridge between rural folk and classic city blues.

Once that bridge was built, Ma Rainey and Bessie Smith made the most of it. Fiercely independent and enormously talented, both Rainey and Smith took classic blues into new areas of personal expression and social commentary. Rainey, who put in twenty years singing with minstrel shows and a traveling circus before recording the blues, was born Gertrude Pridgett in 1886. Except for a few recording sessions, Rainey never sang outside of the South. On many of her recordings she is accompanied by jug, kazoo, washboard, and other improvised folk instruments, but she also recorded with jazz greats Louis Armstrong and Fletcher Henderson. She often selected songs that touched on a wide range of unconventional topics, including poverty, alcoholism, and homosexuality.

Proud and multi-talented, Bessie Smith defined classic blues in the 1920s with her singing and song-writing.

Ma Rainey's most famous student was Bessie Smith. Fifteen years younger than Rainey, Smith also worked with all the leading jazz musicians of her day, and in 1923, her recording of "Down-hearted Blues" sold an astonishing two million copies. But unlike Rainey, Smith also composed, writing such classics as "Poor Man's Blues" and "Back Water Blues," a tribute to the victims of the devastating Mississippi River floods of 1927.

With a violent temper and a sharp tongue, Smith refused to apologize for her bisexual lifestyle or to accept second-class treatment from theater owners or anyone else. These stands gave her a reputation for being difficult and unfairly hurt her career.

Electric-blues master Muddy Waters, one of the leading blues artists since WWII.

Then, with the onset of the Depression, the blues just got too close for comfort for the general public, and Bessie Smith and the blues fell from favor.

Chicago Blues. In the 1940s and 1950s, vast numbers of African-Americans from Mississippi, Texas, and the rural South relocated in California, and in Chicago, Detroit, and other cities of the Midwest. At first, as a side effect of World War II, there were jobs, and conditions seemed brighter than in the impoverished past. Joe Louis was heavyweight champ, and Jackie Robinson broke baseball's color line; each symbolized the hopes for civil rights and equal opportunity.

But these hopes soon faded in the face of the social herding of poor Blacks into African-American ghettos plagued with overcrowding, underfinanced schools, and negligent landlords. Among the many African-Americans suddenly placed into these new hostile surroundings was a talented lineup of blues musicians with colorful nicknames who changed the blues to fit this new life. Some, like Lightnin' Sam Hopkins, stayed close to their folk-blues roots, while Big Joe Turner and others moved in the direction of rhythm and blues, where they were just a short jump away from Chuck Berry, Bo Diddley, and the birth of rock 'n' roll.

Out of Texas came T-Bone Walker and Lightnin' Hopkins. Walker settled in California, became the leader of West Coast blues, and pioneered the electric guitar as a blues instrument. His wild stage antics of doing splits and playing on his knees while leaning over backwards would be copied by Chuck Berry, Elvis Presley, and other rockers. Hopkins, on the other hand, developed a laid-back blues style. On stage, he hardly seemed to be making an effort. But if you looked more closely, his fingers would fly with deft precision as he picked the blues out of his guitar.

Little Walter, Howlin' Wolf, and Muddy Waters all wound up in Chicago, helping to establish it as the blues capital of the world. Little Walter made the harmonica a serious blues instrument, and he invented the technique of cupping his hands around the microphone to play amplified blues harp. Howlin' Wolf had a deep, raspy voice, and his songs took on a menacing sound. But it was Muddy Waters more than anyone else who urbanized the Delta blues. Leaving Mississippi for Chicago, he changed his name from McKinley Morganfield and reinvented himself, abandoning the folk-blues he had recorded in the early 1940s and creating new standards for blues with his slide electric guitar.

The King of the Blues. There were others, such as John Lee Hooker, who was working as a janitor in Detroit in 1948 when he got his first recording contract. But B. B. King is the undisputed King of the Blues. As the blues began to lose its Black fans in the 1960s and 1970s, B. B. King was one of the few musicians who has

Hootchy-Cootchy Woman

Since the classic blues era of Bessie Smith, there have been all too few opportunities for women blues singers. The pattern has been for male singers to sing the blues about women. "Big Time" Sarah Streeter is trying to buck that trend.

Streeter followed the well-worn path from Mississippi to Chicago and spent her weekends as a teen listening to Muddy Waters on Saturday and gospel music on Sunday. The great blues singer Big Mama Thornton was one of her few role models. After twenty years of struggling as a club singer, Streeter has finally received some well-deserved national attention with her 1993 album, *Lay It on 'Em Girls.*

Besides her singing career, Streeter is also dedicated to volunteer work with Chicago's Free Street Organization, a group that helps young people get out of gangs, stay in school, and find jobs.

continued to hold a Black following while introducing a new generation of white fans to his music. Along with the songs of Muddy Waters, his guitar style has greatly influenced white blues greats Johnny Winters, David Bromberg, Paul Butterfield, and the Rolling Stones.

Soul and the Decline of the Blues

Events such as the Chicago Blues Festival remain popular, and blues musicians continue to find small audiences in clubs throughout the U.S. But since the 1970s, blues fans have tended to be white and over thirty, and the blues have failed to recruit new, young talent into its fold. Since the 1960s, the African-American response to racism has shifted from anger, sadness, and resignation to anger, activism, and racial pride. While the blues captured the anguish and alienation of the ghetto, it did not express the hope and community of the Black Power movement. Mixing the singing techniques of the blues with the exuberance of gospel, Otis Redding, James Brown, and Aretha Franklin shaped soul music into the new musical expression of African-American identity. Saying it loud and saying it proud, soul musicians sang about religion, about food, about love and other elements of African-American culture. But as they did so, the folk-blues and spiritual roots of their music became harder and harder to recognize.

World Music and the Future of Folk

Just as there are endangered species, there are endangered musics in our world today. War, politics, economics, and environmental disaster can threaten music as much as it can threaten animal and plant life. When the animals of the rain forest are in jeopardy, so is the music of the people of the rain forest. But there is a growing group of musicians who are dedicated to preserving endangered folk musics and who perform mainstream music that is heavily influenced by music from around the world. They and their fans belong to a loose movement known as world music. In recent years, Paul Simon has merged world rhythms and western pop by featuring South African music on his *Graceland* album and Afro-Brazilian music on *The Rhythm of the Saints*. He has also recently collaborated on a Broadway musical woven around Puerto Rican rhythms and melodies. David Byrne, formerly of The Talking Heads, has similarly featured Brazilian and Cuban music on his recent albums.

All music today comes from other music. If we trace the influences back far enough, we can hear the folk musics of our ancestors. Wherever our people came from, they brought music with them. And when we look for it, we keep that music alive. When we hear it, we listen to ourselves.

Like Peter Gabriel and other proponents of world beat, Paul Simon weaves folk melodies from around the world into his songs.

Music out of this world

When the *Voyager 2* spacecraft was launched in 1977, a special gold-plated, copper record called *The Sounds of Earth* was placed on board. The twenty-seven cuts included music from every continent. Representing the music of North America are "The Navajo Indian Night Chant"; "El Cascabel," performed by Lorenzo Barcelata and the Mariachi Mexico; "Johnny B. Goode," the early rock 'n' roll classic by Chuck Berry; a sensational Chicago jazz tune, "Melancholy Blues," by Louis Armstrong and His Hot Seven; and the haunting Blind Willie Johnson blues song, "Dark Was the Night."

If he could imagine it, he could play it. There was never a more daring and talented jazz musician than Louis Armstrong in his prime.

CHAPTER TWO

Jazz and Music from the Back Alleys

A restaurant in Kansas City, Missouri, 1875. Seated at a table are two European musicians whose paths have crossed many times over the years as they toured the United States and territories giving concerts in barns and music halls, saloons and town squares. One is Ole Bull, the Norwegian violinist, famed for his original compositions and for bringing Mozart to the West. The other is Butler Keane, a trick pianist from Ireland. Keane performs classical and folk compositions but wows his audience by playing with his elbows, his feet, and at least once each performance with his nose. Bull, fresh from a week of sellout shows, is on his way to St. Louis, while Keane has just arrived from Chicago. They take this moment to share dinner and compare notes about their experiences in this fledgling entertainment circuit of the new world.

Keane complains that the competition is getting tough. Everywhere he goes, it seems, there are Swiss yodelers or German beer hall bands or minstrel shows or even traveling revival shows with a full chorus of psalm singers stealing his audiences and making it difficult for him to fill the house when he performs. All of which Bull finds mildly amusing. Smugly, he boasts that wherever he travels, he's still the biggest draw in town. "Except...," he says, then pauses awkwardly wishing he'd never brought it up. But under the influence of his third beer and Keane's prodding, Bull explains. "Except in New Orleans. I just don't understand it. Last month I couldn't draw half the crowds I got down there ten years ago. And get this. Everyone was going across town to hear a nigger fiddler playing some kind of wild and vulgar bush music. Can you imagine that, Butler? Bush music!"

No one knows exactly when or where jazz was born or who invented it. It was a form of music influenced by the past, yet completely different from anything that had gone before it. It was part of something much larger than just music, part of a new way to see reality, something called "modernism" that affected not only music but all the arts. Though it would become commercially popular for a short while, jazz would more often assume the role of "underground" music. But from the alleys and shadows of the U.S., jazz would go on to influence not only pop singers and rap groups, but also symphonic composers, Broadway musical composers, and even poets and writers.

Call and Response

When the British colonies proclaimed their independence and brashly forged an independent nation, music in Africa and music in Europe differed in several important ways. The tension, the interaction, and the blending of these differences would shape and define the development of popular music in the U.S.

The key feature of most African music was drumming. The beating of multiple drums made African music a music of rhythms: complex, interwoven, and hard-driving rhythms. European music, except the folk music of the European peasants, was by contrast a music of sophisticated harmonies. As a result, music in Europe became performance-based. Musicians would perform before large audiences who sat in quiet appreciation, or, perhaps, they danced an elegant dance of formal and restrained movements. But in Africa, music was communal. The whole community would gather and participate, dancing and clapping and shouting in answer to the singing of the leader or leaders, all worked up and wound together by the driving beat of the drums. This basic pattern of the call of the chiefs and the response of the tribe orchestrated the work songs, field hollers, and shouts sung by African-American slaves, and after the abolition of slavery, it greatly influenced the blues, ragtime, and jazz.

The invention of jazz? With the abolition of slavery, African-American musicians swapped techniques and soon developed an early form of jazz.

Abolition and a Burst of Creativity

In addition to striking a great and overdue blow for human freedom, the abolition of slavery in the U.S. let loose a wave of musical creativity that would influence popular music to this day. Musically inclined former slaves were not only free to dedicate more time to their music, but they were also free to travel, to hear other musicians, to pick up techniques and, in turn, to leave their own smudge of influence on the musical communities through which they passed. Until abolition, each plantation developed its own style of slave music influenced by the musical traditions of the region and the heritage of the slaveowner. It was not unusual for French and Spanish music, or church music, or even military marches and classical compositions to have trickled down from "the Big House" to the slaves' quarters. But it was unusual for the music of one slave community to influence the music of another. The music that developed among African-American musicians in the latter half of the nineteenth century, however, was a rapidly changing mix of many styles that had been isolated on plantations for so long. By the end of the century, this music would make its home in the Storyville section of New Orleans and begin a forty-year drive to become the most popular music in the United States. It was called jazz.

The Music of Black Bohemia, Ragtime, and "Pre-Jazz"

You wouldn't find the word *jazz* in a dictionary in 1915. People used it, though. It was slang, a hip synonym for sex. But by 1920, three different strains of music, one from New York City, one from the Mississippi River port town of St. Louis, and one from New Orleans, had come together in Chicago, where fans and musicians first referred to it as jazz.

Before the 1920s, the African-American neighborhood of New York City was known as Black Bohemia. It was centered in West Manhattan around Fifty-third Street, and in the early 1900s, it emerged as the center for some African-American dance orchestras that played a new, hot music. The most famous of these, led by James Reece Europe and Will Marion Cook, introduced early forms of jazz to Carnegie Hall and the Broadway stage. These ensembles were large and consisted mainly of instruments from European orchestras: violins, cellos, mandolins, banjos, and pianos.

Many Europeans got their first taste of jazz during World War I from the U.S. Army's hottest marching band, led by James Reece Europe.

When the U.S. entered World War I, the armed forces were racially segregated, but African-American military bands, because they could jazz up and embroider marching tunes, were often showcased. James Reece Europe directed the U.S. Army's best-known band, and through their performances they introduced jazz to England, France, and much of Europe.

But it wasn't only the music of orchestras and bands that influenced early jazz. Ragtime, a music played on solo piano, became very popular soon after the the turn of the century and had an impact on ensemble jazz and the later jazz-piano styles of stride and boogie-woogie. As the Mississippi River became a major artery of commerce and travel in the late nineteenth century, inns, saloons, gambling houses, and brothels sprang up in ports of call along the way. And almost every one of these establishments hired a piano player to offer patrons musical entertainment.

From among this anonymous legion of "professors and fakers" who could play and improvise virtually anything emerged a man of extraordinary discipline with some very sophisticated ideas about the piano music he was playing. As practiced and preached by Scott Joplin, ragtime was as closely linked to European music as it was to African. Each composition was formally structured, much like a sonata, and designed to be played exactly as written without room for improvisation. The main characteristic of ragtime — syncopation — results when the left hand plays a steady and regular rhythm while the right hand plays a melody that purposely gets ahead of or falls behind the rhythm, before eventually catching up. The result was a jaunty, novel sound that attracted many fans.

The modern-day wonderkid of ragtime

"Never play ragtime fast at any time," warned Scott Joplin (1869-1917). The truth is, not many people could play ragtime at all. Although many bought the sheet music, ragtime proved to be too difficult even for most professional musicians. This did not stop pop music writers from cashing in on the ragtime craze that swept the U.S. from 1905-15, and many songs that were really little more than jazzed-up ballads with piano accompaniment called themselves rags.

The scene now shifts to the 1980s. A high school dropout with no formal musical training composes his first rag before he can read a note of music. He grew up in a family of eight living in the poverty of a three-room apartment in a crime-riddled neighborhood of Chicago's South Side. But as a seventh grader in 1984, he heard a musician play Scott Joplin's "The Entertainer" at his school, and his life was changed.

By the time he was seventeen, Reginald Robinson had taught himself to play piano and read music, and he had composed dozens of intricate ragtime pieces that have the music world whistling in astonishment. Robinson's goal is to get "the whole ragtime thing going again." With such contemporary-sounding rags as "The Hustler's Two-Step" and "Boogie Man Creep," young Robinson may have the genius to do just that.

The popularity of ragtime spread mostly through the sale of sheet music and player-piano rolls, but by the time records became popular in the 1920s, ragtime was already considered quaint and old-fashioned. There were actually more recordings of ragtime in the 1970s after the movie *The Sting* used Joplin's rag "The Entertainer" as its theme song. But ragtime left a legacy of syncopation that became central to the development of jazz, and it helped make the piano a mainstay in future jazz bands.

Storyville, Prostitution, and Hot Jazz

Although the influences from Black Bohemia and ragtime were significant, most of the story of early jazz is set in New Orleans. By the late nineteenth century, New Orleans was a city boasting a gumbo of cultures, and French, Spanish, French-Canadian, American Indian, Caribbean, Creole, and African influences could been seen daily in the makeup of the people, the food, and the music. Although not a society that could boast liberty and justice for all (New Orleans had segregation laws and practices well into the 1950s), no other city in the South offered more diversity and tolerance. Because of this reputation, many freed slaves and African-American musicians were drawn to New Orleans, where they were introduced to new instruments and a community of talented musicians. Without formal training, these self-taught musicians played by ear, often taking a popular tune and embellishing it, coaxing a new range of sounds out of their instruments that formally trained musicians would never attempt.

New Orleans was also a "live-and-let-live" city, and in 1897, the city passed an ordinance legalizing prostitution by restricting it to a section of town known as Storyville. And it was there in Storyville that jazz music found its biggest fans and fertile grounds for development. All the ingredients were there. From the blues came a pinch of African-American folk influence and the techniques of improvisation. From the minstrel shows came the hot rhythms of the cakewalk and dance numbers and the syncopation of the banjo. And from New Orleans itself came the tradition of the European-inspired brass band.

Because of its early association with the red light district and vice center of New Orleans and other cities, some people condemned jazz, just as they had condemned the blues before and as they would later condemn rock and rap,

At a New Orleans funeral, the jazz music of a brass band leads the mourners away from the cemetery and back to life.

branding it "the devil's music." But these detractors had probably never experienced the divinity of a New Orleans funeral. Brass bands had been a part of New Orleans since the French occupation of the territory in the eighteenth century. The bands traditionally consisted of ten to twelve pieces, including at least one trumpet, trombone, tuba, French horn, clarinet, and drums. The brass bands played marches, they played polkas, they played waltzes and mazurkas. But the African-American versions of these bands were best known for their parade music, especially funeral parades. On the way to the graveyard the band would play slow, mournful dirges and understated hymns. On the way back it would start out with a simple snare drum, nothing more. But soon the horns would join in, and with each block farther from the cemetery the music became livelier, faster, wilder. Bystanders would soon join in with the mourners behind the parade, dancing and singing as the band built to a rejoicing crescendo of "When the Saints Go Marching In."

The key feature of this music played in and around Basin Street in Storyville was that it was performed, not composed. Since the music was not written down, it was never played the same way twice. The musicians usually played in groups of five or six, and the main instruments were trumpet, trombone, and clarinet, with support coming from drums, tuba, maybe a banjo or piano, and sometimes a saxophone or bass fiddle. Most of the songs were instrumentals, and the groups did not feature vocalists. Although the groups played a familiar melody at the beginning and end of each song, in between each musician was free to improvise. Only by listening very closely to each other could the members of the group improvise around the unplayed melody so that the music wouldn't degenerate into chaos and they could all get back to playing the melody at the right time.

The legendary horn players from this era were Bunk Johnson, Charles "Buddy" Bolden, Edward "Kid" Ory, and Joe "King" Oliver. Each headed up his own band and enjoyed a good deal of fame. But these were the days before recording contracts, and even the superstars of Storyville had to hold down

Jazz piano and Jelly Roll

Not all of the Storyville jazz greats were horn players. Because the piano was too large for a marching band, it was slow to develop as a central instrument in New Orleans jazz ensembles. But whenever a saloon keeper couldn't afford to hire an entire jazz group, he would hire a piano player. Of all the piano players in Storyville, the undisputed master was Ferdinand Joseph La Menthe Morton. His fans called him Jelly Roll. By playing the piano the way Buddy Bolden played the trumpet, Morton became the first great blues and jazz pianist. Known almost as well for his flamboyant dress and mannerisms, Morton, a Black Creole descended from the Louisiana community of French-speaking African-Americans, was also a composer, and many of his songs such as "Tiger Rag" and "Kansas City Stomp" became big hits.

day jobs to make a living. As musicians, they averaged about two dollars per day, and many doubled as waiters in the clubs where they played.

These horn players competed with each other — in a way that prefigured the famous Battles of the Bands enacted thirty years later in New York City clubs — and spurred their music on to showy, improvisational heights. If any group was drawing larger crowds than his own, Buddy Bolden would set up outside of his rival's club and play his outrageous best until he lured the patrons outside. Then, like the pied piper, he would lead them in parade to the club where his group was playing. A barber by day, Bolden was a true visionary who was a major influence on young Louis Armstrong and on piano great Jelly Roll Morton. Unfortunately, he never took his horn out of New Orleans, and from 1907 until his death in 1931, he was confined to a mental asylum, where he didn't play music at all.

Jazz Music Rides the Illinois Central

Between 1917 and 1920, a series of laws were passed outlawing alcohol in the United States. When federal agents raided Storyville and padlocked the saloons and bordellos, they also played a major hand in moving the jazz capital of the country from New Orleans to Chicago. New Orleans would remain a rich center for music, particularly rhythm and blues and Cajun and zydeco folk musics, and traditional Dixieland jazz would enjoy a revival after the opening of Preservation Hall in 1961. But it would be seventy years before trumpeter Wynton Marsalis and his brothers would once again make New Orleans the fountainhead of cutting-edge jazz.

A speakeasy during prohibition, where people would come to drink illegal whiskey and listen to jazz.

Chicago was not spared from prohibition (the term used to describe the laws making alcohol illegal throughout the U.S. from 1920-33). But politics in Chicago and the influence of powerful racketeers with bootleg liquor interests made prohibition difficult to enforce. Drinks were served in illegal but often elegant clubs called speakeasies, and speakeasies hired musicians. The tracks of the Illinois Central went from the South Side of Chicago to the cabaret district of New Orleans, so it was literally possible for a musician to leave work in New Orleans, walk to the train station, ride to Chicago, and walk to a Chicago club and apply for a job. And for years, the trains had brought Chicago's African-American newspaper, the *Defender*, to southern cities like New Orleans. The *Defender* glorified Chicago, showing it off as a mecca of opportunity and good times for African-Americans, and copies would get passed throughout the Black neighborhoods until they fell apart.

And so they came to the city that would give their music its name and put jazz and jazz musicians in the national spotlight; they came as part of the Great Migration that would resettle millions of African-Americans from the rural South into the urban North; and they blazed a trail that would later be followed by New Orleans bluesmen and more recently by Louisiana Cajun and zydeco musicians. By the early 1920s, dozens of New Orleans stars were working in Chicago. The first jazz record had been recorded, and the city was spawning some very talented white jazz musicians. But the most influential person on the Chicago jazz scene was Louis Armstrong.

The One and Only Satchmo (1900-1971)

Born in New Orleans on the fourth of July, 1900, Daniel Louis Armstrong hardly seemed like the kind of American who would eventually become an internationally known singer, musician, entertainer, and showman; a star of stage, concerts, nightclubs, movies, records, radio, and television; indisputably the one person most identified worldwide with jazz music. His father left his family when Louis was five. At the age of ten, Louis was arrested for firing a handgun, taken away from his mother and sister, and placed in the New Orleans Colored Waifs Home for Boys. At seventeen, while delivering coal to Storyville brothels, he fell for and married a local prostitute, and spent three years in a turbulent marriage that left him angry and depressed.

But he also caught a few breaks. While in reform school, he learned to play bugle and cornet, and as a teenager, he auditioned for Joe "King" Oliver, who liked what he heard and made Armstrong his apprentice. After Oliver

King Oliver's Creole Jazz Band, one of the first great Chicago jazz bands. Joe "King" Oliver, is standing, second from right. A young Louis Armstrong, third from right, stands beside him. Lil Hardin, later Lil Armstrong, is seated at the piano.

took his Creole Jazz Band to Chicago, he asked Armstrong to join him. In 1922, he arrived in Chicago and began an eight-year period of growth and creativity that would change the direction of jazz music and influence every jazz musician since.

Although Oliver was Armstrong's mentor in New Orleans, in Chicago he came under the influence of Lillian Hardin, a classically trained jazz pianist who urged Armstrong to develop his talents as a soloist. A talented musician in her own right, Hardin gave Armstrong a musical education that set his intuitive talents on fire. He began to blow cadenzas from his trumpet unlike anything anyone had ever heard before. Hardin, who in 1924 became Lillian Armstrong, urged Louis to form his own group and to record his music. With the Hot Five and Hot Seven groups on the Okeh label in the late 1920s, Armstrong recorded some of the finest examples of horn playing in the history of jazz. The 1928 recording of "West End Blues" has probably had a greater impact on jazz history than any other song or performance.

Before he left Chicago in 1929, Armstrong made two other contributions to jazz history. According to legend, the first happened accidently during a 1926 recording session when he forgot the lyrics to a song and, without missing a beat, faked it by substituting nonsense syllables. The result was a style of jazz singing called "scat," which uses the voice like an instrument by improvising sounds. Whether by accident or design, scat singing would become one of Armstrong's trademarks, and it would later be practiced and mastered by vocalists such as Ella Fitzgerald and The Manhattan Transfer. The second were the call-and-response improvisations for trumpet and piano that he played with the great Chicago jazz pianist Earl "Fatha" Hines. Piano and trumpet had never before played together as Hines and Armstrong played. Each was at the peak of his talents in the 1920s, and they instinctively inspired each other to new heights of musical wizardry.

After he left Chicago, Armstrong's career as an entertainer and international star kept growing. He went on three world tours, the first in 1932, when he picked up the nickname Satchmo from a British reporter who unflatteringly compared the size of his mouth to a suitcase or satchel. "Satchmo" was a hip, clipped form of "satchel mouth." The name stuck, although later in his career people in the entertainment business affectionately called him "Pops." His popularity peaked in 1964, when he had a superhit with his cover of the Broadway tune "Hello Dolly." Because of his superstar status and his highly visible appearances with Bing Crosby, Frank Sinatra, and other white pop stars in the white-dominated media, Armstrong became a softspoken ambassador for integration in the 1940s and 1950s. But as a jazz musician, he

"Pops" Armstrong, here performing with Bing Crosby, went on to become one of the great entertainers of show business.

would remain content to repeat his work, and he would never again be the innovator and cutting-edge artist that he was during his Chicago era of 1924-29.

Jazz Gets White Hot

Removed from sultry New Orleans and transplanted to the colder, hipper, more hard-boiled and violent ground of Chicago, jazz and the musicians who played it inevitably changed. Gone were any traces of sentimentality or nostalgia for the past. The banjo and the tuba seemed like quaint instruments, and their place in the jazz band gave way to increased emphasis on drums, piano, string bass, and saxophone. And because of virtuosos like Louis Armstrong and those who imitated him, the solos got longer and more improvisational and took up a larger chunk of each song.

One social contribution of Chicago jazz was that it served as the training ground for the first generation of white jazz artists. Led by Italian-Americans Nick La Rocca and Tony Sbarbaro, an all-white five-piece combo calling themselves the Original Dixieland Jass Band (ODJB) stormed the Chicago cafe scene in 1916. Using a cornet-trombone-clarinet front line that would become standard, La Rocca's group was the first to use the word *jazz*

The bright, brief flame of Bix Beiderbecke

Soon after King Oliver and his fellow New Orleans musicians arrived in Chicago and began recording, they inspired a generation of white fans, many of whom dreamed of playing jazz themselves. The white jazzman who was by turns the most resented, admired, praised, and imitated by African-American musicians was Bix Beiderbecke (shown above, second from right, with trombonist Tommy Dorsey).

As a fourteen-year-old in Iowa, Beiderbecke first played cornet when he heard the Original Dixieland Jass Band's records, and he spent hours alone in his room listening to the same records over and over, then trying to imitate the cadenzas of Nick La Rocca. Although he would be dead by the age of twenty-eight, Beiderbecke's records would be studied and copied for two generations. Always reclusive and withdrawn, Beiderbecke was most brilliant during a four-year span in Chicago. No one had ever heard anything like the clear, pure phrasing that he struck from his horn. Although the Chicago bands of this era were racially segregated, Beiderbecke's artistry fired up dreams of integrated bands in which the best musicians, Black and white, could jam together. The color line would be broken in the 1930s, but Beiderbecke would not live to see it. His reclusiveness took a severe, anti-social turn, and he drank alone, continuously, until he died in 1931.

in its name (even though they spelled it "j-a-s-s"). Although they weren't really original, they were good, and they blazed a trail for New Orleans jazz-men in two important ways.

First, the ODJB's music was seen as novelty music, so La Rocca's group competed for bookings with jug bands, Hawaiian bands, "Redskin" bands, and other novelty entertainments. Because they caught on, especially in Chicago, they helped create popular demand for the genuine stuff, and New Orleans musicians no doubt found a friendlier reception as a result. Second, the ODJB was the first group to make a jazz music record with the fledgling record industry. Loud and brassy, jazz worked well with the primitive record technology that lost almost 50 percent of the sound in the recording process.

In 1917, the Victor Company (later known as RCA Victor) tried to persuade the great New Orleans hornman Freddie Keppard to make a record. But Keppard was reluctant, because he feared that a record would allow other musicians to steal his licks. So Victor turned to La Rocca's group, and they recorded Jelly Roll Morton's "Tiger Rag," becoming the first group to make a jazz recording. By the mid-twenties, King Oliver, Kid Ory, and nearly all the New Orleans originals had followed the ODJB to recording studios.

The Charleston, the Dance Bands, and New York Jazz

They were called the "Roaring Twenties" in Chicago. But in New York, the decade preceding the infamous collapse of the stock markets and the world economy was known as the "Jazz Age." Jazz came to represent less a style of music than a way of life. Snake-bitten by the horrors of World War I, many Americans rushed through the 1920s as if each weekend might be their last chance to have a good time. It was a time of outrageous behavior and guilty pleasures. People spoke slang, smoked cigarettes, and drank illegal liquor. Women styled their hair and hemlines shockingly short, and open discussions of sex became commonplace. The excesses of the age are perhaps nowhere better captured than in the novel *The Great Gatsby*, by F. Scott Fitzgerald.

The number-one social activity of the decade was dancing. Those who could afford it frequented glamorous Harlem nightclubs such as the Kentucky Club, the Cotton Club, or Connie's, where they drank bootleg whiskey, listened to a jazz band, and danced the latest hip-wiggling, shoulder-shaking craze: the shimmy, the hootchy-kootchy, the Congeroo, the Black Bottom, the Sugar Foot Strut, the Varsity Drag, and the most famous of all, the Charleston. But it took a lot of green to paint the town red, and not everyone could afford it. Nor was everyone welcomed. Most New York clubs were racially segregated, and in the most famous clubs in the heart of Harlem, the musicians and waiters were Black, but the patrons were strictly white.

Jazz piano, Harlem-style. Willie "The Lion" Smith helped develop stride piano by combining ragtime with jazz.

Rent Parties and Stride Piano

For New York's African-Americans, who had less money and fewer speakeasies to attend than white New Yorkers, the entertainment of choice was the rent party. Rent parties were typically held in an apartment and were open to anyone in the neighborhood who paid the dime or quarter admission. The money was used to hire a piano player, with anything left over going to help pay the rent. These parties are notable because they provided a fertile training ground for a group of piano players who developed what has become known as "Harlem," or stride, piano. The early masters were James P. Johnson and Willie "The Lion" Smith, who converted ragtime into their own brand of New York jazz by speeding up the tempo and incorporating improvisation. But it was a devoted fan of James P. Johnson who became the most famous of the Harlem piano players.

That's funny.
She doesn't look like she can play stride piano.

Stride piano as practiced and perfected by J. P. Johnson and Fats Waller had its heyday in the 1920s and 1930s. This style of playing gets its name because the left hand literally strides back and forth between the left end and the center of the keyboard as it lays down the bass line. This leaves the right hand free to improvise the melody.

The most accomplished stride piano player in the country today is Judy Carmichael, but she's had to break through two stereotypes to get people to take her seriously. Carmichael recalls occasions when people would show up at a club where she was scheduled to play, see a skinny white woman at the piano, figure there must be some mistake, and leave. To make matters worse, Judy doesn't sing, and the public has come to expect female performers to sing first and maybe fool around with an instrument on the side. But Carmichael has overcome these restrictions. When it comes to contemporary stride piano, jazz critics today consider her the keeper of the flame.

Fats Waller, who went on to become a star of stage and screen, cut his teeth playing piano at Harlem rent parties.

Playing the rent-party circuit and writing songs that suited his "shout" style of singing, Thomas Wright "Fats" Waller both played the piano and lived his life with wild abandon. By 1925, so great was his reputation as an entertainer that the Chicago mobster Al Capone had his henchmen abduct Waller at gunpoint and bring him to Chicago where he was obliged to play a command performance for the gangster before being paid handsomely and released. Fast living and overindulgence in food and drink contributed to his early death from bronchial pneumonia at the age of thirty-nine, but his talent and musical influence reached far beyond the piano parties of his youth. Fats Waller went on to appear in films, write the musical score for Broadway plays, perform at Carnegie Hall, and compose over three hundred songs. Among the Waller tunes that are still popular today are "Ain't Misbehavin'," "Sunny Side of the Street" (which he sold for drink money), and the blues song about discrimination, "What Did I Do To Be So Black and Blue?"

Big Band Jazz and the Rise of Swing

Outside of this tiny but talent-packed circle of rent parties, U.S. music of the 1920s and 1930s was dominated by the dance band, and bandleaders, not musicians, were the stars of the entertainment world. New York City was the center of this industry, but there were about fifty thousand such orchestras nationwide. Although few of these were true jazz bands, most were jazz-influenced, and the media and the general public thought of their music as jazz. Many bandleaders brought the influence of their own ethnic backgrounds to this spectrum of American pop-jazz. There was Cuban-American Vincent Lopez, Jewish-Americans Ben Bernie and Ben Pollack, Italian-American Ted Fiorito, Italian-Canadian Guy Lombardo, African-American Cab Calloway, French-born immigrant Jean Goldkette, and Irish-Americans

Cuban-American bandleader Vincent Lopez ignited the 1920s' dance band craze.

Tommy and Jimmy Dorsey, just to name a few. As is all too often the case, however, the artists who made the most lasting and important contributions to jazz are not the same ones who enjoyed the financial rewards and fame.

African-American Fletcher Henderson came to New York City from Atlanta to do postgraduate work in chemistry. But he unexpectedly switched his attention to music and played a key role in adapting jazz from the five-piece Chicago ensemble to the eleven- to fifteen-piece big band. A pianist, arranger, businessman, and jazz visionary, it was Henderson who first organized the jazz band into sections — the saxophone section, the trombone section, the trumpet section, and the rhythm section (piano, bass, drums, and sometimes guitar). The new sound resulted from the call and response of sections rather than of soloists. There was still improvisation, but with more musicians improvisation risked chaos and breakdown, so the roles of the bandleader and of the arranger became very important.

Henderson's orchestra played the prestigious Roseland Ballroom throughout much of the 1920s and 1930s and featured some great soloists, including saxophonists Coleman Hawkins and Don Redmon, who went on to become a great arranger in his own right. But when times got tough in the Depression, Henderson couldn't afford to keep his band together. He spent the next fifteen years working as an arranger behind the scenes to help create the successful sound for swing superbands led by Benny Goodman, Tommy Dorsey, and others.

Duke Ellington and the Harlem Renaissance

Henderson not only innovated new musical styles, he also led the way for a host of African-American jazz bands, notably those led by Chick Webb, Charlie Barnet, and Jimmie Lunceford, and helped create a brief boom period of opportunity for African-American musicians. Of the many jazz artists who

The devil's music

Not everyone was a jazz fan in the the 1920s. One educator warned, "Its influence is as harmful and degrading to the civilized races as it has always been among savages from whom we borrowed it." And a physician gave this medical opinion: "Jazz affects the brain through the sense of hearing, giving the same results as alcoholic drinks taken into the system." In a sermon, Reverend John Roach Straton condemned jazz as a music of "spiritual debauchery, utter degradation," and the Christian and Missionary Alliance Conference adopted a resolution declaring that "American girls are maturing too quickly under the hectic influence of jazz."

At the same time, the critic Hiram Motherwell was one of the first to see jazz as art, calling it "the perfect expression of the American city, with its restless bustle and motion, its multitude of unrelated details, and its underlying rhythmic progress towards a vague Somewhere."

benefited from that opportunity, one went on to become the most famous of all bandleaders and the most accomplished composer in American music history: he was Edward Kennedy "Duke" Ellington.

Ellington played piano, but his real instrument was his orchestra, a group he put together in the mid-1920s and kept together for an astounding fifty years. They stayed with him because he paid them well, gave them good parts to play, and always maintained an elegant and debonair image for himself and his orchestra, refusing to submit to the pressures of the white-controlled media that urged African-American entertainers to roll their eyes, show their pearly whites, or even wear jungle loincloths to mug for the cameras. There were no vestiges of the minstrel show in Duke Ellington's Orchestra.

After a stable childhood in Washington, D.C., where his chief interests were baseball and art, Ellington sought

his fate as a musician in New York. This was about the same time that talented African-Americans from throughout the South left their homes, crisscrossed America, and found each other in the New York City neighborhood of Harlem. Together with Ellington and other African-American musicians, poet Langston Hughes, novelist Zora Neale Hurston, and essayist James Weldon Johnson led an exciting artistic community that has come to be known as the Harlem Renaissance.

Top: Composer, bandleader, and musician Duke Ellington at the piano with his orchestra. In a career that spanned six decades, Ellington broadened the range of jazz more than any other artist. *Bottom:* The New York neighborhood of Harlem, home to the famous Cotton Club and a community of African-American artists in the 1920s and 1930s, a time known as the Harlem Renaissance.

Jungle Jazz and the Cotton Club

Even earlier in his career Ellington was expanding the vocabulary of jazz, creating new sounds from his orchestra and giving expression to an ever-widening spectrum of feelings and emotions. Ellington got his first big break after hooking up with Irving Mills, a down-on-his-luck Jewish music publisher who became Ellington's business manager. Needless to say, this was Mills's big break, too. In December of 1927, Mills got Ellington booked as the headliner in Harlem's hottest nightspot, the Cotton Club. It was here that Ellington wowed audiences with "East St. Louis Toodle-Oo," "Creole Love Call," and other songs characterized by innovative growls and sneers coaxed from the trombone and trumpet sections. Although the critics labeled this "jungle music," and the racist term stuck for a while, Ellington refused to let

The Cotton Club, one of the hottest night-clubs in Harlem, showcased many of the best jazz bands in New York but would not admit Black customers.

his music settle into a formula. Through live radio broadcasts, motion picture appearances, national and European tours, and concert hall performances, Ellington introduced jazz audiences to an incredible variety of new sounds. These included jazz songs that used a concerto format and Latin jazz, especially in hits such as "Caravan" and "Perdido" that featured Puerto Rican trombonist Juan Tizol.

Before he died in 1974, Duke Ellington received over one hundred major awards from nations and artistic organizations around the world. Along the way, he was not only an artistic pioneer, but with the help of the business-wise Irving Mills, Ellington became one of the first African-American musicians to appeal to both white and Black audiences, to retain the publishing rights to his songs, and to tour the country successfully and comfortably during the segregated and economically hard-pressed 1930s.

It Don't Mean a Thing If It Ain't Got That Swing

Although Duke Ellington's song "It Don't Mean A Thing If It Ain't Got That Swing" helped boost the popularity of swing, Ellington's orchestra never really became a swing band, and their decision not to jump on this "bandwag-on" led to their fall from popularity in the 1940s. Swing's roots can be traced back to the late 1920s with Fletcher Henderson's band, but it wasn't until 1935, when Fascist armies in Spain, Italy, and Germany were pushing the world to the brink of war and nine million Americans had lost their life savings in U.S. bank failures, that swing captured the imagination of a Depression-weary public to become an overnight sensation.

With unemployment rampant and wages at an all-time low, Americans across the U.S. were selling apples, shining shoes, turning to petty crime, scrambling to make a living any way they could. In an effort to restore some feeling of economic and social dignity, Franklin D. Roosevelt created hundreds of thousands of jobs paying a dollar a day plus room and board and also delivered on a promise to repeal prohibition. As a result, speakeasies and nightclubs were replaced by dance halls and stage shows as the arena for big bands. The best of these bands also found their way to the big screen of movies, the big broadcast of radio, and the big experiment of juke boxes. Performing for larger if poorer audiences, the bands became brassier, their beat more driving.

Unlike the plaintive folk-blues of Leadbelly and Robert Johnson that captured the agonies of these times, swing music offered an escape. Flashy, loud, and upbeat, swing was a variation of New Orleans jazz that used strong, driving rhythms and racing horns and clarinets with carefully structured arrangements. In most bands, the musicians had to know how to read music, and they improvised only when the arrangement called for it. In a bow to showmanship, the band often wore costumes of colorful, satin tuxedos, the drum set was elevated and emblazoned with the band's logo, and entire sections would stand up in unison in the middle of a song when it was their turn to take the lead.

From the Synagogue to Carnegie Hall

The musician most identified with swing music is the clarinet-playing bandleader Benny Goodman. Goodman not only perfected swing as a popular art form, he was also instrumental in assisting the careers of Count Basie, Billie Holiday, and Fletcher Henderson. He also helped break down the racial barriers that existed in the music world of the 1930s. As one of eleven children of an impoverished Jewish family living in a Chicago ghetto, Goodman began playing the clarinet with a boys' band from the neighborhood synagogue. Though he never turned his back on his classical training and would go on to record the definitive take on Mozart's Clarinet Concerto, Goodman taught himself jazz by listening to records, and he found his clarinet was his ticket out of the ghetto. By the 1920s, he was playing with Red Nichols and His Five Pennies, perhaps the best white jazz band in the country at the time. Actually a ten-piece band, the Five Pennies also included youngsters Jimmy Dorsey and Glenn Miller, each of whom went on to be famous swing band leaders.

Clarinetist and bandleader Benny Goodman, the King of Swing and agent of racial integration in the music world who got his start as a boy with a band in a Chicago synagogue.

By 1934, Goodman was leading his own orchestra, but they played a bland style of sweet dance music and were virtual unknowns until he made two decisive moves. He hired Fletcher Henderson to write big band arrangements of New Orleans jazz classics for his group, and he signed up Gene Krupa as his drummer. Along with African-American bandleader Chick Webb, Krupa revolutionized the role of jazz drummer, changing it from the musician who kept time for the band to featured soloist. With Henderson's arrangements and Krupa's driving drumplay, Goodman stunned a national audience with a series of live radio broadcasts in 1935 that made swing the music of choice and catapulted Goodman and his orchestra to stardom.

In 1936, they played the Paramount Theater in New York City, where the youthful audience went wild, prefiguring the hysteria later generated by Frank Sinatra, Elvis Presley, and the Beatles. A year later, for an older and calmer but equally appreciative audience, Goodman and his orchestra presented a swing program in Carnegie Hall. Then, just when he reached the top of the pop music world, Goodman risked it all by recruiting African-American musicians Lionel Hampton on vibraphone and Teddy Wilson on piano and making them featured soloists in the orchestra.

Breaking the Color Line

White and African-American jazz artists had gotten together for private jams and recording sessions as early as the late 1920s, and in 1929, no less of a talent than Louis Armstrong made some notable recordings with the young Tommy

Verboten! "Niggerjazz" and the Nazis

After several European tours in the 1920s and 1930s by jazz notables such as Louis Armstrong and Duke Ellington, American jazz won many fans throughout Europe and especially in Germany, much to the horror of Adolf Hitler and his Nazi cohorts. With hot rhythms and free, improvisational forms, swing music and jazz were the exact opposite of the goosestep marching music that captured the spirit of the Third Reich. But even more infuriating to the Fascist regime was that so many master jazz musicians were African-American, Jewish, or otherwise non-"Aryan" and so challenged the idea of the "master race" on which they based their politics.

In 1935, the Third Reich outlawed "niggerjazz," declaring it contrary to the National Socialist (Nazi) spirit. Musicians who played swing were subject to three years of hard labor in a concentration camp, and people caught listening to the British broadcasts of jazz that jammed the German airwaves were whisked away in a Black Maria patrol wagon and often never heard from again.

Below: Despite suffering from tuberculosis of the spine, bandleader Chick Webb was one of the most dazzling jazz drummers of the 1930s. *Bottom:* The Savoy Ballroom, with its gymnasium-size dance floor, was the site of many wild "Battles of the Bands."

and Jimmy Dorsey, an experience that contributed significantly to their development as jazz musicians.

But Goodman's orchestra was the first major act to give live, integrated performances, and they did so at a time when pro baseball and football teams were racially segregated, when African-Americans could not serve on juries in many states, and where throughout the South strict segregation laws were a way of life. In later years, Goodman frequently teamed up with Count Basie, and some unforgettable recordings resulted when Basie and Goodman formed a combo of musicians from each of their bands.

Goodman and his orchestra were also key players in the integration of jazz one night in 1937, when they showed up at the Savoy Ballroom in Harlem to challenge Chick Webb and his orchestra to a good-natured "battle of the bands." In contests such as this bands would set up stages on opposite ends of a dancefloor and alternate songs, driving each other on to wilder heights of virtuosity, finally letting the audience decide who had "won." Although primarily an African-American haunt, the Savoy was known as one of the first nightspots to welcome patrons of all races. On this particular night, five thousand fans jammed onto the two hundred by fifty-foot dance floor to enjoy a four-hour fest that finally ended when a Chick Webb drum solo had Goodman and Gene Krupa shaking their heads in disbelief. But the real winners were all jazz fans who benefited from the swapping of musical ideas in this new interracial musical community.

World War II and the End of Swing

Although Benny Goodman continued to perform into the 1980s, he never entirely abandoned swing. But with the outbreak of World War II, swing music suddenly seemed inappropriate and frivolous as a popular art form. Between gas rationing and the draft, there weren't enough qualified musicians left to staff all the big bands, and there wasn't enough gasoline to allow big bands to go on tour. The war was serious, and all Americans were asked to make sacrifices. Families and couples were broken up as soldiers were sent overseas to serve in the war effort and face possible death, a point tragically brought home when bandleader Glenn Miller died as his plane was shot down over the English Channel. On the home front, curfews, amusement taxes, and a ban on recording emphasized that popular entertainment must serve in the war effort. Despite the maverick "Uncle Sam Blues," a song by Hot Lips Page that begins with the plaint, "Uncle Sam ain't no woman, but he sure can take your man away," the new popular songs were ballads such as "Don't Sit Under the Apple Tree with Anyone Else But Me," a more patriotic if less passionate tune about willingly parted lovers who hope to be reunited after the war.

Glenn Miller (foreground) led one of the last big swing bands before he died in WWII.

With the breakup of the big bands into smaller jazz combos, the musicians, known as sidemen, scattered. Some, like Louis Jordan and Illinois Jacquet, broke with jazz and helped to develop the hard-honking sounds of rhythm and blues that soon gave rise to rock 'n' roll. Others, including Dizzy Gillespie, took jazz into a strange land of highly improvisational, non-melody-based jazz that came to be known as bebop.

Count Basie brought the "jump" to swing. His band showcased a legion of talented sidemen who emerged as great soloists in their own right.

Basie's Men

A few soloists emerged from the anonymous legions of sidemen to make contributions worth mentioning. The violin was all but ignored as a jazz instrument until Italian-American Joe Venuti virtually reinvented how to play it. And Gypsy jazz guitarist Django Reinhardt merged European folk, flamenco, and American jazz into a unique playing style. But probably no band produced more significant soloists than the Count Basie Orchestra.

After studying at the elbow of Fats Waller and playing with the great Midwest bandleader Bennie Moten, William "Count" Basie led his own band in 1935 and developed a variation of swing called "jump." With more improvisation and longer solos in Basie's band than in any other band of the 1930s and 1940s, many great soloists developed their artistry by following Basie's direction to "find your own notes."

The Lady Who Swings the Band

Except for several all-women novelty bands, U.S. society and the jazz community provided virtually no encouragement for women

Mary Lou Williams blazed a path in jazz for women composers and instrumentalists.

instrumentalists. It would wait until the 1980s and 1990s before this began to change. But organist and quartet-leader Shirley Scott, trumpeter Rebecca Coupe Franks, saxophonists Jane Ira Bloom and Virginia Mayhew, pianist Joann Brackeen, drummers Candy Finch and Cindy Blackman, and other critically acclaimed women virtuosos of today owe a debt of gratitude to trailblazer Mary Lou Williams (1910-1981). Mary Lou Williams was not a singer, she was not sexy or sultry, and she did not wear slinky, glittering dresses on stage. She was a strong, two-handed piano player and talented composer and arranger. Her musical career blossomed in the swing era when she performed with the Andy Kirk band, but it spanned six decades and touched upon every jazz style from ragtime and Dixieland to bebop and beyond. At various times, she wrote arrangements for Tommy Dorsey, Duke Ellington, and Jimmie Lunceford. But perhaps she made her most significant contributions from her Harlem apartment, where she held court and over the years took under her wing such jazz artists as Benny Goodman, Errcll Garner, Thelonius Monk, Mel Torme, and Miles Davis. As a composer, Williams rivaled Duke Ellington. She left over 350 compositions, including several jazz masses and the "Zodiac Suite," a sophisticated twelve-part jazz interpretation that has been performed by the New York Philharmonic Orchestra.

Featured Vocalists, Torch Singers, and Billie Holiday

The one area where women jazz artists excelled and continue to excel today is singing. In the big band and swing era, the featured vocalist was second only to the bandleader in star status. Among the star singers were Mildred Bailey, the first white singer to win acclaim as a jazz vocalist, and African-Americans

Billie "Lady Day" Holiday, widely regarded as the most gifted jazz singer of all time.

Ivie Anderson and Ella Fitzgerald, as well as crossover blues artists Bessie Smith, Mamie Smith, Ethel Waters, and Ma Rainey. But no one could use her voice like a muted cornet better than Billie Holiday. When Billie sang, she usually slowed down the tempo and shaped the song with subtle phrases of melody.

Billie Holiday's life was as filled with horror as her singing was filled with beauty. Born in Baltimore to a thirteen-year-old mother in 1915, she was raised in abject poverty. At the age of six, she was blamed for her grandmother's death. At the age of ten, a man tried to rape her. When she reported it to the police, she was arrested and charged with "enticement." At the age of twelve, Billie, in an orphanage, was punished by being locked in a room with a dead girl. With this kind of childhood, it is little wonder that she spent the rest of her life battling addictions to drugs, alcohol, food, and abusive relationships. She was arrested many times, usually for possession of narcotics, and in 1947, the authorities took away her cabaret license, which means she couldn't sing anywhere liquor was served. The last time she was arrested was on her deathbed in 1959. Even when she was out of jail, performing and temporarily drug-free, Holiday was plagued by insecurities, and she was never confident of her own immense talents.

But everyone else recognized her artistry. She sang with Count Basie, Benny Goodman, and Artie Shaw. With Shaw's orchestra, Holiday was the first African-American singer to tour the South with a white band, and for several years she was the featured performer at Barney Josephson's Cafe Society, one of the first integrated nightclubs in New York City. Her relentless persecution by the law was no doubt due not just to her drug use but to her visibility as a pioneer of integrated entertainment.

For all of her talent and accomplishments, Billie Holiday never received much financial reward. From 1933-44, she recorded over two hundred songs, each for a flat fee of about fifty dollars. Some of these, especially those like "God Bless the Child," "My Man," "Ain't Nobody's Business," and "Strange Fruit," songs that expressed the pain of her personal life, went on to become classics of American jazz. Yet Holiday never received any royalties. And like all too many musical artists, she has gotten more recognition since her death than during her lifetime.

Bebop and Beyond

After World War II, most Americans, eager to put the brutal disruptions of war and economic hardship behind them, rushed headlong into a life of conformity. Move to the suburbs, curse the Russians, buy a TV, love your car, and hum along with the pretty and polished sentimental ballads that made the

Pioneers of bebop jazz Charlie Parker and Dizzy Gillespie.

hit parade. A fine formula if you were more concerned with material well-being than with racial integration and social justice. But led by a small group of virtuoso, African-American musicians, jazz took a sharp turn and developed a revolutionary new style. It was called bebop, and it was a music of rebellion. It rebelled against swing and all that it had come to represent: the rigid structure of arranged music, the dominance of melody to ensure commercial success, and the authority of a bandleader. Perhaps most of all it was a music of rebellion against middle-class values and way of life.

Bebop began in the early 1940s at Minton's, a Harlem nightclub, where three young and virtually unknown geniuses played together and changed the course of jazz history. Piano player Thelonius Monk, trumpeter Dizzy Gillespie, and saxophonist Charlie Parker were each dissatisfied with the creative opportunities of big band jazz, and when they got together, they shifted jazz from dance music to listening music and returned it to the small combo. Their music was softer, quieter, but at the same time more complex and intricate. Vocals, if any at all, were often scat nonsense syllables; or, as in the case of Gillespie's 1942 composition "Salt Peanuts," words were used not for their sense but for their sound. Bebop was difficult to play, and only a few people appreciated it. In a slur that he may have later regretted, Louis Armstrong dismissed the new jazz as "Chinese music."

But the new bebop combos played for small, appreciative audiences in dark and intimate settings. Bop musicians and their fans became recognizable by their sunglasses at night, their berets and, for the men, goatee beards — and by the hip, slang language understood only by insiders of the bebop culture. Ten years later, bebop had become the jazz of choice for the community of Anglo-American bohemians. The media would label this "the beatnik culture," and it would represent the extremes of nonconformity in the 1950s.

Bird Calls

Miles Davis, one of the most respected modern jazz trumpeters, once said, "The history of jazz can be told in four words: Louis Armstrong, Charlie Parker." Even though his career was cut short by an early death, saxophonist Charlie "Bird" Parker distinguished himself as the most creative improvisational jazz musician of all time. Along with Monk, Gillespie, guitarist Charlie Christian, and drummer Kenny Clark, Parker formed the first bebop combo, and in 1945, he and Gillespie released the first bebop records, "Koko" and "Shaw 'Nuff."

Like Billie Holiday, Bird was a great artist whose life was dissipated and made miserable by self-destructive behavior and substance abuse. By the time he came from Kansas City to Manhattan as a teenager, he brought a heroin habit with him. The next fifteen years were spent alternating bursts of creativity with periods of imprisonment and hospitalization. When he died in 1955 at the age of thirty-four, his heart, liver, and lungs were in such poor condition from alcohol and drug abuse that the coroner estimated his age at fifty-five. A poor businessman, Parker was often taken advantage of, and many of his compositions were copyrighted by pirates. He died penniless, but twenty years later he won a Grammy when his early 1940s recordings were rereleased.

Miles Davis, who later experimented with jazz-rock fusion.

From Bebop to World Jazz

Bebop never captured the audience that swing enjoyed, but it freed jazz from the restrictions that are the price of commercial success. Once bebop opened the doors, jazz underwent a rapid series of new styles and experimentation. Cool jazz, third stream, free jazz, fusion, and modern big band all drew upon the influence of bebop and in turn have influenced one another. Jazz today often picks and chooses elements from all of these styles and mixes it with a good dose of traditional jazz. Since bebop, jazz has continued to be dominated by African-American musicians and composers. Many of them have borrowed from classical and non-European traditions, and today jazz increasingly shows the international influence of world music.

One area of modern jazz that has served surprisingly well as a multicultural vehicle is the modern big band. Ellington and Basie never completely disbanded their groups, and they were joined by Anglo-American bandleaders Don Ellis, Stan Kenton, and Woody Herman. Of all the big bands, African-American Sun Ra and and the Solar Arkestra have been the most avant-garde.

In recent years, increasing numbers of Latin and Asian-Americans have risen through the jazz ranks, and they have brought with them a musical heritage that is helping to develop a world jazz. The music of Machito and his Afro-Cuban Orchestra, the Chico O'Farill Orchestra, and Tito Puente have introduced jazz fans and other jazz musicians to the rhythms of salsa, Caribbean, and South American jazz. And tenor sax player Stan Getz helped make Brazilian-inspired jazz popular as early as the 1970s, when he brought guitarist Joao Gilberto and percussionist Airto Morcira into his group. Truly innovative and captivating is the combination of modern big band sounds with elements from Oriental music created by the band led by Japanese-American Toshiko Akiyoshi. And trumpeter Terumasa Hino, saxophonist Sadao Watanabe, pianist Yosuke Yamashita, and guitarist Akio Sosajima are among the most exciting young jazz soloists playing today.

The hundred-year history of jazz is not just a history of a musical style. It is also the story of modern America. From the seedy alleys of New Orleans, to the stage in Avery Fisher Hall at Lincoln Center, through two world wars and a Depression: it is the story of the creative spirit of those ethnically diverse Americans who are most often the victims of bias, discrimination, and injustice. It's why we snap our fingers and tap our feet and how we get through hard times.

A typical skit from the longest-running entertainment in nineteenth-century America, the minstrel show.

CHAPTER THREE

Mainstream Pop
and the Music Business

Twenty-eighth Street, New York City, 1915. It looks like any other commercial avenue in the city, except here the pedestrians are showered with
the plink-plank-plunking of two dozen pianos, each playing a different song,
and a chorus of off-key singers belting out a cacophony of moons, croons,
spoons, and Junes. This is Tin Pan Alley, and its business is music. In office
after office in the buildings on this street, America's music publishers and
their hired guns grind out songs by the dozens in hopes of scoring with the
year's big hit and making a small fortune. In every room is a piano, sometimes
two, and hunched over each are one or two or three men working on a song.

L. Wolfe Gilbert, an immigrant Jew from Odessa, Ukraine, sits at a piano
by the window of a second-story office. Like so many of the nine million
Europeans who came to the U.S. since the early 1900s, Gilbert found the
doors closed to most jobs in business, banking, law, and medicine. But the
entertainment business wasn't concerned with his nationality. All that
mattered was whether he could write songs, good songs, songs that would sell.

That he could do. Gilbert's background was steeped in the rhythms of the
Yiddish language and the melodies of "dovening" the prayers of the synagogue. But that's not what his song is about. Today he writes a song about
the South, about steamboats, about the past. "Dixie" songs had been popular
ever since the minstrel shows of the 1800s, and they continued to be in vogue
in the twentieth. He writes a song about levees in Alabammy and calls it
"Waitin' for the Robert E. Lee," even though he's never been on a steamship
and there are no levees in Alabama. L. Wolfe Gilbert is an Alleyman.

The Business of Music Begins

Before records, before tapes and CDs, before radio, before MTV, there was a
music business. And what a business it was: ethnically and racially diverse and
filled with talented, colorful personalities, classic American success stories,
and dramatic falls into oblivion. It was a business based on selling sheet music,

The first part, or "olio," of a minstrel show with white performers in blackface. Note the endmen Mr. Bones (left), on bones, and Mr. Tambo (right), on tambourine.

the popularity of home pianos, and live performances by traveling entertainers.

Many runaway smash hits of the 1800s became children's songs of the 1900s and are still taught in schools and recorded today, including "The Blue Tail Fly (Jimmy Crack Corn)," "Dixie," "The Old Folks at Home (Swanee River)," "Oh! Susanna," "Buffalo Gals," "Polly Wolly Doodle," "Camptown Races," and "Old Black Joe." These songs and hundreds like them were popularized by the writers and performers of the first form of mass entertainment in the U.S.: the minstrel show.

Mr. Bones, Mr. Tambo, and the Minstrel Show

Minstrel shows began in the 1840s, and soon there were dozens of successful minstrel troupes touring the U.S. and Europe. The Virginia Minstrels, under the direction of Dan Emmett, were the first, and they set the basic formula that all others followed. Until after the Civil War, a minstrel show consisted of white performers who blackened their faces with burnt cork, drew red and white circles around their lips to make them look larger, and presented an evening of songs, dances, and jokes in a stereotyped imitation of African-American slaves entertaining themselves on the plantation. Two stereotypes emerged early on, became stock characters of the minstrel show for seventy-five years, and persisted into the Hollywood era and to some extent even today. One was the joyous, ragged, and rugged field hand Gumbo Chaff or Jim Crow. The other was called Zip Coon or Dandy Jim — the citified northern Negro, impeccably costumed in flashy clothes and exaggerated mannerisms.

Looking back, the whole concept strikes us as so racist and in such patently poor taste that it is a wonder that the troupes were so popular. But America, at the time, was a nation struggling with its own conscience over slavery. On the one hand, it was a way of life, and without it, the economy of the southern states would fall apart. On the other, the outrage of the abolitionists had struck a chord in the hearts of most Americans in the northern states, and the issue would soon divide the nation in war. The minstrel shows very likely calmed the nation's guilty conscience by portraying African-Americans as happy-go-lucky slaves. Such highly romanticized parodies left the audience sympathetic to the caricatures but out of touch with the terrible plight of the true slaves. A comfortable feeling for the American who opposed slavery but didn't want to actually do anything about it.

Despite this, the minstrel shows gave Americans their first pleasant earful of African-American music, even though it was a watered-down imitation.

The music of minstrel shows would eventually be a major influence on vaudeville, ragtime, the Broadway musical, and even jazz. The first shows were performed by four players on stage: the banjo and fiddle player in the middle, the tambourine and bones player on either end. The bones player literally played bones, clacking them together as a primitive percussion instrument. Although later troupes had as many as several dozens of performers on stage at one time, the American minstrel show stuck with the basic three-act structure introduced by Emmett and perfected by the most famous minstrel of all, E. P. Christy. The first part, or "olio," featured dances and songs in between the banter of jokes and riddles between the two end men, Mr. Bones and Mr. Tambo. The second part, or fantasia, was more free form, with each entertainer performing his specialty. The third part consisted of comic skits and satirical monologues and was called the burlesque.

Following the Civil War and the abolition of slavery, slave humor lost much of its relevance. Taking advantage of the recent wave of immigration from Ireland and Germany, minstrel songwriters thus turned their talents to lyrics that parodied Irish, German, and Yiddish characters, dialects, and accents. But the most significant innovations in minstrelsy after the Civil War were the introduction of African-American and integrated minstrel troupes. By the time the Georgia Minstrels became the first all-Black group of its kind, the tradition of performing in blackface had become so accepted that the performers applied the burnt cork in an odd spectacle of African-Americans imitating Anglo-Americans imitating African-Americans. Even so, much of the caricature started by Emmett and Christy gradually gave way to renditions of more authentic African-American comedy, song, and dance. It was during this period that James A. Bland became the first African-American pop-song composer. Writing for Black minstrel troupes, Bland penned such late-nineteenth-century hits as "Hand Me Down My Walking Cane" and "Carry Me Back to Old Virginny," which years later was adopted as the official song of the state of Virginia.

The first integrated minstrel troupe, The Forty Whites and Thirty Blacks, debuted in 1893, just three years before the U.S. Supreme Court would rule (*Plessy v. Ferguson*) that enforced racial segregation was constitutional. And although minstrel troupes never recaptured the popularity they enjoyed before the Civil War, some companies survived well into the twentieth century. Al Jolson and Lew Dockstader, who would go on to star in vaudeville, on Broadway, and in the movies, got their start in latter-day minstrel shows. And future blues and jazz artists W. C. Handy, Ma Rainey, Jelly Roll Morton, Bunk Johnson, and Lester Young all cut their teeth with minstrel troupes.

There's No Business But Show Business

As the minstrel troupes declined in popularity after 1880, a huge wave of twenty million Europeans began arriving in the U.S. Although the Statue of Liberty, unveiled in 1886, officially welcomed these immigrants from Ireland, Italy, and Eastern European Jewish ghettos, unofficially they were greeted with suspicion and hostility. As Americans adjusted to life after the

Civil War, jobs were scarce, the frontier was disappearing, and these "foreigners" were unfairly judged as dangerous rejects from their old countries. This fear of foreigners that swept the country was known as xenophobia, and it even affected immigrants who had arrived a generation before and who now turned their backs on Europeans following in their footsteps.

So, shunned by the mainstream of U.S. society, this new generation of immigrants was forced to turn to the fringe professions to earn a living, and many found a place as singers, songwriters, and song-peddlers in the growing world of show business. The most popular form of live entertainment at the turn of the century was vaudeville and its cousins, the revue and the burlesque show. Vaudeville was made up of several large regional chains of theaters, such as the Orpheum circuit in the West and the United Booking circuit in the East. Singers, dancers, comedians, and other stage entertainers would travel from theater to theater, putting on family-oriented variety shows. Vaudeville made singers into stars and songs into hits.

"Coon" Songs and Stereotypes

The songs themselves were very sentimental and filled with stereotypes. One of the most popular types of songs was the "coon" song. Performed equally by African-Americans and by whites in blackface, six hundred of these songs were published between 1890 and 1900, the same years that saw a dramatic increase in the African-American population of the urban North. Many, such as "The Laughing Coon" and "Nobody," became huge hits. Racist relics of the minstrel show, these songs combined plantation dialects with stereotyped images of ham bones and possum meat in otherwise sympathetic ballads of brazen lovers and broken hearts. The new immigrants didn't fare much better. These weren't hate songs in any sense, but they reinforced stereotypes. The Irish were portrayed as working stiffs who loved a good fight, while Germans loved to drink beer to the background of band music. And Jews were comically portrayed as cheapskates and pawn-shop usurers.

Although many of the singing stars of vaudeville were women, the songs themselves almost always portrayed women within one of several cliched stereotypes. There were "mammies," which included not only the heavy-set plantation mother with a bandanna on her head, but also the Jewish momma and mom from mainstream America. Then, there were the "red-hot mommas." These were not mothers but robust older women with outspoken sexual appetites. A subtler, more slender, but more lethal version was known as the "vamp." Finally, on the more wholesome side, there was the "old-fashioned girl" and her kid sister, the "All-American kiddo." With some variation, all of these stereotypes unfortunately linger in popular song lyrics of today.

Singers, Songwriters, and Pluggers

Vaudeville reached its peak of popularity in the years 1910-20. The Marx Brothers, Jimmy Durante, Bill "Bojangles" Robinson, Harry Houdini, and George Burns and Gracie Allen all first reached stardom in vaudeville before going on to further success on Broadway, in Hollywood, and even on TV. For them and so many others, vaudeville was their ticket out of the ghetto or the poor rural South and into mainstream America. Among the many African-American comic singers who achieved stardom were Bert Williams and ex-slave George Washington Johnson. Jewish immigrants Sophie Tucker and Emma Carus were among the first of the red-hot mommas. Many other Jewish singers, including Al Jolson, Nora Bayes, and Belle Baker, anglicized their names to disguise their ethnic identity, but then turned around

and went public with such songs as "Eilu Eilu" (a part-Yiddish showstopper) and the comic "Cohen Owes Me Ninety-seven Dollars." Despite the tendency not to challenge public prejudices, no place in America could boast as much diversity as the vaudeville community.

At its peak, there were over one thousand vaudeville theaters in the U.S. An entire industry of professional songwriters arose to supply tunes to vaudeville stars and then to sell copies of the sheet music to millions of piano-playing Americans when the songs became hits. After Charles K. Harris took his "Songs Made To Order" shingle with him from Milwaukee to NYC and became the founding father of Tin Pan Alley, the industry became dominated by European ethnics until it was eventually broken up by Hollywood, Nashville, and rock 'n' roll.

While many Americans may not have thought too highly of the nation's growing Jewish population, they were whistling the songs of its writers. African-American rhythms also found their way into mainstream music through Tin Pan Alley. Composer and piano player Ben Harney popularized ragtime with such hits as "Mister Johnson, Turn Me Loose." A light-skinned Black man, Harney hid his racial identity and spent most of his life passing for white. Later composers, such as the team of Henry Creamer and Turner Layton, made no such pretenses, although few Americans realized the authors of "If You Knew Susie" were Black. By the 1920s, however, W. C. Handy had come to Tin Pan Alley, and the blues replaced "coon" songs as a more authentic expression of popular Black music.

The business side of Tin Pan Alley cared more about selling songs than creating them. From 1890 to 1920, songs made money for their publishers through the sales of sheet music and player-piano rolls. Player pianos were invented about the same time as record players, but phonographs did not catch on with the public until the 1920s. Piano rolls were rolled sheets of paper with perforations that made the piano play a song by itself. All the player had to do was pump foot pedals.

A hit song could make a lot of money. Sheet music averaged about fifty cents, and piano rolls sold for about two dollars. A hit could easily sell one million copies of sheet music and one hundred thousand piano

Carrie Jacobs Bond: move over, Irving Berlin

Before Judy Collins, Joni Mitchell, and the era of the singer-composer that began in the 1960s, women songwriters were given little encouragement or professional opportunity. But at a time when women in the U.S. were still denied the right to vote, a young widow in Chicago overcame the odds to establish herself as a successful and admired songwriter.

Carrie Jacobs Bond ran a boarding house in Chicago, and when her songs kept getting rejected by Tin Pan Alley publishers, she converted one of her spare bedrooms into an office, fought off her disappointment, and set up her own music firm, The Bond Shop. Her talent lay in romantic ballads, and among her biggest hits are "I Love You Truly" and "A Perfect Day." Soon a celebrity, Jacobs Bond continued composing for Hollywood and performing her songs until her death in 1946.

Monkeying around with the music business

One of the most daring and ingenious promotional ideas in the music business came from an anonymous plugger around the turn of the century. He made a business arrangement with a New York City Italian *padrone*. The *padrone* was a community leader who would help newly arrived Italian families get settled and find work. Among other things, the *padrone* also decided who would get to be the organ grinders in the neighborhoods he controlled.

The organ grinder was once a common sight on the sidewalks of New York. He held a hand-cranked box organ that played a song while a trained monkey with a cup would collect tips from passersby. By arrangement with the *padrone*, and for a price, all the organ grinders' organs were playing the plugger's songs. Soon thousands of New Yorkers were wondering, "What is that song I'm humming, and where have I heard it before?"

rolls. Charles K. Harris, the Milwaukeean who started it all, sold ten million copies of the sheet music of his big hit, "After the Ball." With this kind of money at stake, publishers were reluctant to leave the fate of a song to chance, so they hired a staff of people, very often immigrants and second-generation ethnics, whose job it was to promote the songs their employer published. They were known as pluggers, and they would do almost anything from singing songs in department stores to wining, dining, and even bribing vaudeville singers to use a particular song in their act. By the 1950s and 1960s, this extended to influencing radio disc jockeys in their choice of songs to play, and when it erupted as the "payola" scandal, many a career was ruined. Pop music giants Irving Berlin, Jerome Kern, and George Gershwin all got their start in music as pluggers.

Broadway: The Diversity of the Great White Way

Another source of many smash hit songs from the late 1800s through today has been the Broadway musical. Because the Puritans and other European colonists considered plays immoral, musical theater was slow to develop in the U.S., and the first shows were disguised as "lectures with music." By the mid-1800s, however, musical theater was coming out of the closet, particularly in New York City, with a vengeance. The chief attraction of Broadway's first hit musical, *The Black Crook* (1866), appears to have been the un-Puritan sight of women in tights on stage.

Musical styles from throughout Europe contributed to the shaping of the Broadway musical. Their influence left a heavy European stamp on the stage and stifled the development of more democratic theater by using most-

Tin Pan Alley goes to war

When in 1914 Europe exploded in war, the whole messy affair seemed far away from the U.S. The year 1916 saw the worst military carnage in the history of the world as hundreds of thousands of Europeans died in the Battle of the Somme, but the big craze in U.S. music was for Hawaiian songs about hula girls who could "yacki, hacki, wicki, wacki, woo." But the next year, when the U.S. joined the fray, a huge propaganda campaign was launched, and Tin Pan Alley was quick to play its part in the war effort.

With its usual mix of wit and cliche, Tin Pan Alleymen wrote about the war from the foot soldier's point of view and came up with such hits as "If He Can Fight Like He Can Love, Goodnight Germany" and "Would You Rather Be a Colonel with an Eagle on Your Shoulder or a Private with a Chicken on Your Knee?" But peace songs were forbidden, and even the operas of German composer Richard Wagner were banned from U.S. performances.

ly aristocratic characters and plots set in foreign lands in the distant past. It wasn't until composers and writers borrowed elements from the minstrel show and the Yiddish theater of the Ashkenazi Jewish community that they hit upon the formula of using recognizable characters who sang songs that the audience could take home with them.

The Mulligan Guard Ball (1879) was the first musical set in New York City using Irish, German, and African-American characters, but it was Irish-American George M. Cohan who snapped off the American musical from its European models. A song-and-dance man on the vaudeville circuit, Cohan became the most successful composer in the years 1900-20. His trademark was snappy, often patriotic tunes, and in hit shows such as *Forty-five Minutes from Broadway* and *George Washington, Jr.*, Cohan debuted hit tunes "Give My Regards to Broadway," "You're a Grand Old Flag," "Yankee Doodle Boy," and others. It was also Cohan who wrote "Over There," the song that served as the rallying anthem for the U.S. when it entered World War I.

African-Americans on Broadway

The first Black character to appear on the American stage came from *The Padlock*, an early nineteenth century ballad opera. This unrealistic character with the unrealistic name of Mungo was played by a white actor in blackface. In 1896, *Oriental America* premiered as the first Broadway show with an all African-American cast, and there soon followed a flurry of Broadway musicals written by and for African-Americans. Orchestra leader and composer Will Marion Cook helped bring early forms of jazz to the Broadway stage with a half dozen smash hits, including *In Dahomey* (1902) and *In Bandana Land* (1907). At the same time, Robert Cole teamed with James Weldon Johnson and his brother J. Rosamund Johnson to write the musicals *The Shoo-Fly Regiment* (1906) and *The Red Moon* (1908). Although these plays were performed almost exclusively for white audiences, they made a significant break from the stereotypes of the minstrel show and provided

Irish-American composer George M. Cohan (below), the first to write Broadway musicals with a distinctly American flavor. Among his many patriotic tunes is "Over There" (bottom), a rallying song for Americans during WWI.

opportunity for many talented African-American performers. The popularity and artistic sophistication of African-American Broadway musicals soared in the 1920s. In 1921, jazz and ragtime piano player Eubie Blake teamed with lyricist Noble Sissle for *Shuffle Along*, the first of four Blake-Sissle hit shows. Josephine Baker and Paul Robeson, both of whom soon left the United States to escape racism and seek artistic freedom in Europe, starred in the show, which helped spark the period of African-American creativity known as the Harlem Renaissance. Twenty-seven years later, when Harry Truman barely beat Thomas Dewey in the presidential election, he may have owed his narrow victory to the popularity of his campaign theme song, "I'm Just Wild About Harry," from *Shuffle Along*.

Above: Exotic singer and actress Josephine Baker starred with Paul Robeson in the African-American Broadway play *Shuffle Along*.

Below: Jewish-American songwriting team George and Ira Gershwin broke new ground on Broadway with *Porgy and Bess*, which combined African-American folk melodies with opera.

White Composers Steal the Spotlight

By the time stride piano player Fats Waller broke attendance records with his pop-jazz tunes in *Hot Chocolates* (1929), the African-American Broadway musical was proof of the abundance of African-American singers, dancers, actors, and composers. It was also a proven formula for commercial success. Soon white composers were writing musicals for all-Black casts and imitating African-American musical styles. Both "Old Man River" and "Summertime," two songs most identified with the African-American stage, were written by white composers. The first is from Jerome Kern's *Showboat* (1927), the second from George Gershwin's *Porgy and Bess* (1935). And both Kern and Gershwin owe part of their enormous success to the influence of spirituals, blues, jazz, and other African-American styles.

As Kern and Gershwin were joined by Cole Porter, Irving Berlin, the team of Richard Rodgers and Oscar Hammerstein, and others in composing African-American-influenced musicals, there was less of the real thing. During the Depression, all-Black musicals were restricted to low-budget movies that never found a wide audience. In 1947, the great African-American writer Langston Hughes teamed with Kurt Weill to produce *Street Scene*, a musical about tenement life in NYC. And in 1975, *The Wizard of Oz* was rewritten as *The Wiz*, a Motown-styled musical with Harlem replacing Kansas. But for the most part, since the Depression African-American musicals have been limited to all-Black productions of proven hits such as the Pearl Bailey-Cab Calloway version of *Hello Dolly* and revues such as *Sophisticated Ladies, Ain't Misbehavin', Five Guys Named Moe,* and *Jelly's Last Jam.* Though these lavish revivals keep the music of jazz greats Duke Ellington, Fats Waller, Louis Jordan, and Jelly Roll Morton fresh, they do little to bring the sting of contemporary issues and musical styles to the Black stage.

The Rise of Records, Radio, and Big Bucks

Broadway and Tin Pan Alley remained the main sources of hit songs until rock and country took over the pop charts in the

Jewish-American innovators on Broadway

All too often, Broadway musicals fall into a rut. Since they cost so much to make and the people who put up the money prefer not to take big risks, it is unusual for a musical to strike out in daring new directions. But thanks largely to a talented group of composers, many of them Jewish-American, the American musical stage has been pushed beyond the bland and predictable formula into new realms of creativity.

In 1931, the Jewish-American foursome of George and Ira Gershwin, George Kaufman, and Morrie Ryskind used elements of fantasy to create a satire of patriotism called *Of Thee I Sing.* Several years later, after spending months among African-American fieldworkers in South Carolina, George Gershwin combined African-American folk music with opera to create *Porgy and Bess.*

Twenty-two years later, symphony orchestra conductor and composer Leonard Bernstein joined Jerome Robbins to produce another musical that broke all the rules. Set among rival Italian and Puerto Rican teen gangs in New York City, *West Side Story* retells the tale of Romeo and Juliet. Combining modern ballet with operatic duets, Latin rhythms, and jazz, Bernstein and Robbins created a work that is equally at home on Broadway and in the concert hall.

1960s and 1970s. And then the live stage gave way to records and radio as the force that made songs into hits and singers into stars. Broadcast and recording technologies made music into big business. And with big business came, in the interest of making big money, the need to appeal to the most people. This meant mass-producing songs that were pretty, polished, and bland. But every time the industry thought it had found the perfect formula, a large portion of the public just wouldn't buy it. Instead, they would "discover" hillbilly songs, or the blues, or doo-wop, or rap, or some other music that had been flourishing in the corners of our culture.

The Early Days of Records. The first two record companies, Columbia and Victor, started in the 1890s with the idea of bringing classical music to the masses. But in 1900, when they had their first hit records on their hands, to their surprise it was the laughing and whistling "coon" songs of ex-slave and vaudevillian George Washington Johnson. It wasn't until twenty years later, with the rise of dance music and Chicagoland jazz, that records really caught on with the public and for the first time began to outsell sheet music. When, in 1920, African-American Mamie Smith belted out a raspy rendition of "Crazy Blues" for a new label, Okeh records, the industry had its first disc that sold one hundred thousand copies (at almost one dollar apiece!).

But Smith's hit also began the ghettoization of African-American music by the record companies. As the number of records increased, the companies divided all their records into three groups: hillbilly, race, and everything else. The hillbilly section included all country and white folk music, including the immensely popular "yodeling" tunes of Jimmie Rodgers. Rodgers, who didn't start recording until he was dying of tuberculosis, sold twenty million records in the late 1920s and early 1930s. But so regional was his appeal that he remained unknown to most of the U.S. The race section covered blues, hot jazz, and Black folk and spirituals. The companies spent most of their money producing and promoting "everything else," however, and this included dance orchestra music and ballads sung by white crooners. Okeh had the largest race selection, but record sales slumped seriously in the Depression-era thirties, and for most of the decade African-American music flourished quietly in the shadows of mainstream music. It wasn't until after WWII with the rise of independent record labels such as Decca, Atlantic, and Chess that avenues opened up once again for African-American artists.

The Rise of Radio. In 1920, when KDKA in Pittsburgh became America's first radio station, it began a revolution in the music business. By 1929, there were three hundred radio stations that regularly broadcast music across the U.S. At the same time, record sales, which had peaked at 110 million in 1922, fell to fewer than one million ten years later. As the U.S. fell into the Great Depression, Americans turned to radio, where music was free. All you had to do was listen to some jingles about the sponsor's product. Problem was, sometimes it was hard to tell the difference between a commercial jingle and a hit tune, a compromising fuzziness that persists today.

Radio made stars of dozens of bandleaders. In 1921, Cuban-American Vincent Lopez set the mold when he and his orchestra broadcast live from the Pennsylvania Grill in New York City, sparking both the dance-band craze and the popularity of radio. And radio turned singers into superstars and teen idols. Rudy Vallee and later Bing Crosby set the standards for the ballad-singing crooner, and in the 1930s, sixty million Americans tuned in weekly to Kate Smith's radio show. Because radio could make a hit in seven days and turn it into an oldie in sixty, there was more need than ever for a continuous flow of fresh new songs. All of these stars and songs should have made conditions ripe for greater diversity and variety in popular music.

Radio Limits Diversity. But it wasn't to be. One reason for the lack of variety in radio: because radio technology was best suited to capture the high fidelity sound within a limited scale of five notes, the many songs written for radio sounded great, but they were limited to this scale and were thus intentionally bland. Second, though there were many radio stations, until the 1940s 88 percent of them were owned by two networks, NBC and CBS, and sponsors discouraged programming that was too experimental. In 1929, the networks adopted a code of ethics that banned songs with sexual or political lyrics. Unfortunately, this excluded most blues and jazz from the playlists — even though the very first banned song was a Tin Pan Alley novelty ditty, "How Could Red Riding Hood Have Been So Very Good and Still Keep the Wolf from the Door?" Cole Porter's "Love for Sale" was allowed, but only as an instrumental.

The Jukebox and a Comeback for Diversity

Within a few years, however, partly as a byproduct of greed, the doors of pop music were suddenly opened wide. Thanks to a rivalry between two groups in the music business — one made

With her booming voice and inspirational songs, Kate Smith was the most popular entertainer in America during the Depression.

up of music artists and publishers, the other of broadcasters — radio found itself looking for ways to cash in on a wider listening audience. It did this by broadcasting music that was heavily flavored with blues, jazz, country, and folk.

Then, in the 1940s, just as the economy was recovering and for the first time in ten years Americans had some change in their pockets, Decca led a host of new, independent record companies by introducing the thirty-five cent record and recording lots of blues, jazz, and other neglected African-American music. Swing music became enormously popular and also helped the resurgence of record sales. But perhaps the greatest contribution to the diversification of pop music in the 1940s was the miniature temple of chrome and lights known as the jukebox. In the rural South of the 1930s, Black bars that offered musical entertainment were known as "jukes," and the first juke boxes appeared in 1933. By 1939, there were 225,000 of them, not only in southern saloons and honky-tonks, but also in luncheonettes, drug stores, and railroad stations across the U.S. People cued up songs to fit their moods, five cents a play, six for a quarter. And for the first time since the rise of radio, hit songs were determined in part by the nickel vote of the public and not by the promotional push of the sponsor.

Playing the Game: TV and Music Videos

From Dan Emmett and Al Jolson, through the Andrews Sisters and Frank Sinatra, to Michael Jackson, Mariah Carey, and En Vogue, pop music stars in the U.S. have had to play the music business game. At first it was minstrelsy and vaudeville, later Broadway, radio, and records. Today it is music videos.

In the 1950s and 1960s, popular shows like "American Bandstand," "Soul Train," and even "Hee Haw" gave increased *visual* exposure to music and helped push rock 'n' roll, soul, and country into the mainstream of *pop* rock, *pop* rhythm and blues, and *pop* country. With MTV, the Black Entertainment Network, the Nashville Network, and other music programming, a music *video* is now required for a song to be a hit, for a singer to be a star. Songs without videos simply don't climb to the top of the pop charts anymore. But videos are expensive to produce. The most costly, such as *Thriller* and others by Michael Jackson, have production budgets in excess of one million dollars.

While music videos bring pop music performances to life, they also ring in a new age of popular music that is predictable and mainstream. For every music video we see, how many other songs, full of ethnic creativity and vital diversity, are being sung in the alleys and bushes far from the cameras and cash registers of the music business?

Dick Clark's daily TV show, "American Bandstand," helped popularize rock 'n' roll in the 1950s and 1960s. Clark (center) also greatly influenced the style of rock 'n' roll, nudging it from its cultural roots into the mainstream of pop music.

The Godfather of Soul. With an electrifying stage show and hits like "I Feel Good," James Brown staked his claim in the 1960s to being "Soul Brother Number One."

CHAPTER FOUR

Rock 'n' Roll
and the Rhythms of the Street

Cleveland, Ohio, 1952. The first day of spring. Judging from the morning paper, which prominently features coverage of the international communist conspiracy, stories of juvenile delinquents and vandalism, and a cautionary report about the rise of venereal disease among Cleveland teenagers, it's hard for the adults to tell who's the bigger headache: the commies or the town teens. But for twenty-five thousand or more Cleveland teens, all but a few of them African-Americans, the challenge of the day is figuring out how to get out of the house and into the Cleveland Arena tonight for The Moondog Coronation Ball.

The brainchild of Alan Freed, the half-Jewish, half-Welsh disc jockey whose radio show broadcasts the rhythm and blues and doo-wop that other stations won't play, the Coronation Ball is the first event of its kind. African-American teens from miles around have jammed downtown Cleveland to pay the $1.50 admission to see and hear Paul "Hucklebuck" Williams, Tiny Grimes and the Rockin' Highlanders, The Dominoes, and other performers of songs that even Cleveland's African-American newspaper, the *Call and Post*, calls music of "bum taste, low morality and downright gutbucket subversions." But there's something about the driving beat, the honking sax, and the screaming vocals that expresses the feelings of a new generation of Americans.

The crowds are so large and so excited that the doors to the arena cannot open fast enough or wide enough. No sooner does Hucklebuck take the stage and start his lusty, honkin' rendition of his hit, "Thirty-five Thirty," than the entire arena erupts into a wild, swirling pulse of dance. Still trying to get in, the crowd outside breaks down the front doors and sets off a wave of pushing and shoving that laps right up to the stage. To the authorities, it looks like a mob of Blacks on the verge of a riot, and they're not far from wrong. So they blow their whistles, storm the arena, and shut the show down tight. But the doors of the Cleveland Arena this night are the doors of musical history. And

The Moondog himself. DJ Alan Freed, whose 1950s radio and stage shows championed early rock 'n' roll.

through those doors blow the winds that link the music of the future with the music of the past.

Rock performers of today — whether they are innovative or traditional, heavy metal or hip-hop, garage or grunge — play in reaction to and influenced by earlier rock artists, who reacted against or were influenced by Chuck Berry, Little Richard, and the first generation of rock 'n' rollers, who were influenced by Louis Jordan and the rhythm and bluesmen, who were reacting to the decadence of big band jazz and influenced by boogie-woogie, which grew out of Dixieland jazz and country blues, which drew upon the field songs of slaves and the folk melodies that the colonists brought with them from Europe. And so it is that a line can be traced — a twisted and snaky and looping line, but an unbroken line — from the minstrel shows, Story-ville, and Tin Pan Alley to Smashing Pumpkins, Arrested Development, and Snoop Doggy Dogg.

The African-American Roots of Rock 'n' Roll

So much of our life has been enriched by the customs, arts, and contributions of African-Americans. Time and time again, when popular music lapsed into the doldrums, the industry would look to the rural South and the urban ghettos of the North to see what was cooking in "race" music, meaning what records Blacks were buying. Then they would copy a bit of this, a bit of that, watering down and changing anything they felt was "unclean," taking just enough to spiff up pop music and pop music sales, but rarely giving credit to the original Black artists. To some extent, George Gershwin, Benny Goodman, Sophie Tucker, and Frank Sinatra each profited greatly by bringing African-American rhythms from the musical ghettos into the mainstream. But even though this was a common practice, the history of the U.S.A. has rarely witnessed an act of cultural larceny as outrageous as white America's takeover of rock 'n' roll.

The rock 'n' roll classic "Shake, Rattle, and Roll" is a case in point. "Big Joe" Turner, a blues shouter from Kansas City who sang with Count Basie and other bands in the 1930s and 1940s, cut "Shake, Rattle, and Roll" for a small, independent company, Atlantic Records, in 1954. As Eddie "Cleanhead" Vinson and other blues singers were unemployed and fading from public memory, Turner, in his forties, mixed up solid dance rhythms with blues and boogie-woogie to help create a new musical style. The song sold well in the African-American neighborhoods, what the record industry called the "R & B" market, but it never made the pop charts, and to this day there are few people who have ever heard Turner's original of this history-making rock 'n' roll song. Instead, most people know the version by Bill Haley and the Comets, recorded later that same year. In Haley's version, known as a "cover," the opening line "Get out of that bed and wash yo' face and hands" is changed to "Get out in that kitchen and rattle those pots and pans." All the lyrics that were considered too lusty were changed, but the rhythm and the catchy

Rockabilly sensations Bill Haley (center) and the Comets mixed country music with rhythm and blues.

chorus were kept, giving Haley a big hit and helping to make him one of the first superstars of rock 'n' roll.

Rhythm and Blues and Neglected Hormones

When conditions after World War II virtually put an end to big band music and swing, the void was filled by pop crooners such as Perry Como and Patti Page and by the underground of bebop jazz. Although this development satisfied the conformists and noncomformists of the adult world, America's teens were cheated. You couldn't dance to bebop, and although the pop singers had great voices, they were backed by bland, anonymous studio

The Dance Sensation that's sweepin' the nation

They did the Slop and the Mashed Potatoes, they danced the Swim and the Stroll. They Limboed and they Monkeyed, and oh how they Frugged! They danced the Loco-Motion, the Watusi, the Chicken and the Fly, the Jerk, the Hitchhiker, the Pony and the Popeye. The decade of the 1960s saw more dance crazes than any time since the 1920s. But the craziest craze of them all was the Twist.

"The Twist" was written and originally recorded in 1959 by Hank Ballard, a talented R & B artist. Dick Clark, host of "American Bandstand," liked the song. But he didn't like Ballard, whose reputation was built on risque songs such as "Work with Me Annie" and whose image was not clean-cut enough for Clark's show. So in 1960, Clark found an African-American teenager from Philadelphia who had a knack for imitating the pop singers of the day. He could do everyone from Elvis Presley and Fats Domino to the Chipmunks. And he could do Hank Ballard. His name was Ernest Evans, but the world came to know him as

Chubby Checker, a variant of "Fats Domino" suggested by Dick Clark's wife. And so "The Twist," by Chubby Checker (shown here with Clark and country rocker Conway Twitty), became the number-one song. Soon everyone — from the Mouseketeers to Jackie Kennedy — was twisting the night away. And Hank Ballard? He was quite happy with the royalties he earned for having written the song. And eventually, he crossed into the pop charts with a hit of his own, "Finger Poppin' Time."

musicians, and the result was strictly mellowsville. Big deal? *Very* big deal. In twentieth-century America, dancing had become a ritual, the ritual, by which teens of all races came to meet other teens. Through dancing, they learned to strut their stuff, and at dances they eased the awkwardness of learning romance.

Who wrote the book of love? Well, in the years after WWII, it was African-American musicians, such as Louis Jordan, the Dominoes, and Ruth Brown, who took a third path, playing a new dance music that soon gave rise to rock 'n' roll.

Today, rhythm and blues, or "R & B," is a catch-all label for a wide variety of music from Janet Jackson to Michael Bolton. But historically, R & B refers to a very specific music that evolved in the 1940s and early 1950s. It was the blues set to dance music. It mixed up boogie-woogie and gospel with a tenor sax, an electric guitar, and a shout style of singing. It wasn't played much on radio, and songs were recorded in makeshift studios set up in garages and backrooms. But it got discovered anyway, and it became the music for a generation of American teens.

Louis Jordan pioneered R & B when the industry was still calling it "race" music. Like thousands of other talented musicians, Jordan's career as a sideman for various big bands was suddenly jeopardized when swing no longer meant a thing. But with a stroke of genius and good luck, Jordan formed a small combo called the Tympany Five. Their music was like the blues, but the lyrics often were humorous. It wasn't swing, but you could dance to it. And their songs were popular with both Blacks and whites. Between 1944 and 1949, Jordan and his Tympany Five scored with "Open the Door, Richard," "Choo-Choo Ch'Boogie," and seventeen other hits that crossed over to the pop charts. Jordan was a model for Chuck Berry, Bill Haley, Little Richard, and other first-generation rock 'n' rollers.

African-American women also pioneered the raw, snarling rhythm and blues that led to rock 'n' roll. Willie Mae "Big Mama" Thornton is probably best known as the original singer of "Hound Dog," the song that made Elvis Presley a national teenage idol. Thornton's version, which made number one on the R & B charts in 1953, is a woman's declaration of independence. "You ain't nothin' but a hound dog," she chides her shiftless man, "I ain't gonna feed you no more." Sadly, Thornton died impoverished in a Los Angeles boarding house, but her music went on to influence not only the first female rock 'n' rollers, Ruth Brown and LaVern Baker, but also Janis Joplin and Aretha Franklin.

Your rock 'n' roll resume looks a little spotty

What they did before rock 'n' roll catapulted them into stardom:

Elvis Presley	movie usher, lawn mower, truck driver, factory hand
Fats Domino	bedspring factory worker, lumber mill worker
Chuck Berry	hairdresser
Bo Diddley	boxer, sheriff
Little Richard	snake-oil pitchman, dishwasher
Dave Clark	movie stuntman
Berry Gordy, Jr.	Ford assembly-line worker
Chubby Checker	chicken plucker
Janis Joplin	hooker

Led by Tony Williams and Zola Taylor, the Platters mastered the silky harmonies of doo-wop in the 1950s.

Street Corner Harmonies and Doo-Wop

In 1948, Baltimore was a segregated city. Theaters and public swimming pools regularly posted "Whites Only" signs, and "No Jews Allowed" shingles were common. But that year, a young Jewish woman and five African-American men put their musical and business talents together to change the course of musical history. The men were a talented singing group known as the Orioles. The woman, Deborah Chessler, was their manager and songwriter.

Before 1948, Chessler was a sales clerk and each of the five Orioles held down menial day jobs while trying to book weekend singing engagements. But then Chessler wrote "It's Too Soon to Know." With lead singer Sonny Til's emotional interpretation, the song soared to number one on the R & B charts. There was never anything quite like it before, and the record became the standard of doo-wop, an R & B style characterized not by the shout, the snarl, and the honk, but by silky vocal harmonies.

Doo-wop groups took their cue from the Mills Brothers and the Ink Spots, successful recording artists of the 1930s and 1940s who harmonized and used their voices to make the sounds of instruments. By the early 1950s, groups of young African-Americans in cities across the country were singing on street corners and rehearsing in school stairwells, which gave them a nice echo effect. After a series of hits for the Orioles, many groups imitated not only their sound, but also their name. There were the Flamingoes, the Robins, the Swallows, the Larks, and groups named for nearly every bird in the birdhouse. But the most successful were the Drifters, led by Clyde McPhatter, who scored with such hits as "Save the Last Dance for Me" and who were the first doo-wop group with a Latin musical influence; the Platters, with lead singer Tony Williams and hits such as "Only You" and "The Great Pretender"; and later doo-wop groups such as the Shirelles, an all-female trio from Newark led by Shirley Owens, and the kings of Italian-American doo-wop, Dion and the Belmonts. The Dell-Vikings were notable not only for their big hit, "Come Go with Me," but also for being the first racially integrated doo-wop group.

Although the Coasters returned the humor and honk of Louis Jordan to join R & B with doo-wop in "Charlie Brown," "Yakety Yak," and other

> Ginger bread, ginger bread, ginger bread, ginger bread,
> ginger bread, ginger bread, ginger bread, ginger bread,
> you're full of sugar, you're full of spice,
> you're kind of naughty but you're naughty and nice.
> — "Ginger Bread"
> (Clint Ballard, Jr., and Hank Hunter)

Above: By the end of the 1950s, R & B fans scratched their heads as Annette Funicello and Frankie Avalon led teen rock to the top of the charts.

Opposite: Three who shaped early rock 'n' roll: Jerry Lee Lewis (top), who mixed country with gospel; Texas rockabilly genius Buddy Holly (center); and Mexican-American rocker Ritchie Valens (bottom), who scored big mixing rock 'n' roll with a Mexican folk tune in "La Bamba."

classics, most doo-wop songs were about angels, dreams, and moonlight, and were characterized by the soft, sentimental feelings of love and sadness, often sung in falsetto harmonies. They may have been singing on the corners, but odds are they were crying in the chapel before the second verse. Doo-wop, of course, went on to influence the Temptations, the Four Tops, the Supremes, and other Motown greats, and an updated nineties version called hip-hop doo-wop is beautifully practiced by groups such as Shai, Silk, Jodeci, Tony Toni Tone, and Boyz II Men.

From R & B to Rock 'n' Roll

Frankie Avalon's "Ginger Bread," a typical rock 'n' roll hit at the end of the 1950s, was a far cry from the Dominoes' "Sixty Minute Man," one of the rollicking R & B sides that opened the decade. Critics of this "teen rock" that had taken over claimed the songs of white teen idols Avalon, Bobby Rydell ("Wild One"), and Mouseketeer graduate Annette Funicello ("Tall Paul") were more white bread than gingerbread or pumpernickel. It would take an invasion of British rockers in the mid-1960s to bring the blues back to American rock 'n' roll. But how R & B became rock 'n' roll is a both a marketing story and a musical one. And it involves some of the best musicians, white and Black, in the history of American music.

Rhythm and blues was a term the record industry made up to market music in African-American neighborhoods without calling it by the more offensive term, "race" music. Few expected that white teens in significant numbers would listen to African-American disc jockeys broadcasting R & B in cities across the country. In these days before chain stores, local record shop owners were the first to notice white teens with dollar bills stride right past the neat stacks of Victor, Columbia, and Capitol records they were "supposed" to buy to snatch up the latest R & B releases on the Chess, Savoy, or Peacock labels. Tipped off by one such record shop owner, Alan Freed became the first non-Black deejay not only to play but to promote R & B to an integrated audience. First in Cleveland, then later in New York City, Freed became a star and a hero to millions of teens for playing the music they wanted to hear and producing live stage shows that drew thousands. But if the music was to be actively marketed to European-American teens, then it wouldn't do to keep calling it rhythm and blues, which in 1950s America still meant "Negro music." The phrase "rock and roll" had appeared in the lyrics of a dozen or so songs of the late forties and early fifties (usually, like "jazz" beforehand, as a synonym for sex). But it was Freed who popularized the term "rock 'n' roll" as a kind of music.

One-Two-Three O'Clock, Four O'Clock Rock

But it was *The Blackboard Jungle*, a 1955 movie about juvenile delinquents at a tech high school, that turned rock 'n' roll into a battle cry. The soundtrack featured the song "Rock Around the Clock" by a white country combo, Bill Haley and the Comets. The song became an anthem for a generation of rebels without a cause and turned the unlikely Haley, a pudgy father of five, into rock 'n' roll's first idol. Haley was trained in country music, and he earned his stripes by playing dives for a dollar a night when he billed himself as the Ramblin' Yodeler. But as early as 1950, he was drawn to rhythm and blues, and soon he was writing songs in that style such as "Crazy, Man, Crazy" and "Rock-a-Beatin' Boogie." The result, the first of its kind, was rockabilly, an early form of rock 'n' roll that blended country with R & B.

Throughout the 1950s, many white male country musicians followed Haley's lead, recording some of the great hits of the decade. Carl Perkins, who stayed closest to the country tradition, is reputed to have written "Blue Suede Shoes" on a potato sack at three o'clock one morning. Jerry Lee Lewis, on the other hand, strayed farthest from his country roots. Singing with the fervor of a gospel preacher and assaulting his piano, Lewis gave us the wild classics "Great Balls of Fire" and "Whole Lotta Shakin' Goin' On." Texan Buddy Holly, who died at the age of twenty-one in the same plane crash that took Ritchie Valens and the Big Bopper, scored big with "Peggy Sue" and "That'll Be the Day." Fifties rock 'n' roll also gave us "Wake Up Little Susie" and "Bird Dog" from the Opry-trained Everly Brothers, and young Ricky Nelson's hits, "I'm Walkin'" and "Be-Bop Baby." And into the sixties, Roy Orbison continued the rockabilly tradition with "In Dreams" and "Crying." But no one defined the spirit of rock 'n' roll in the 1950s more than Elvis Presley.

The White Boy Who Could Sing Colored

Within the span of just a few months in 1956, millions of American teens had a shared experience. They sat with their parents watching Tommy Dorsey, Milton Berle, or Ed Sullivan's family-oriented variety show on TV, when on came a rock 'n' roll singer with a sneer on his lips and his eyes half-closed, calling a woman "a nuth thin buttah houn' dog," using "ain't," and twitching his hips like he was romancing his guitar, on the verge of losing control as he sang (omigod!) *wild Negro music*. Parental reaction was varied, ranging from mild amusement to turning off the TV in disgust to clasping their Perry Como records to their chests and muttering "please let it be a passing fad."

Even before Elvis Presley, rock 'n' roll had established itself as the first music written by young Americans and sung by young Americans to an audience of young Americans. But with Elvis, rock

'n' roll became style, posture, and attitude; it became a way of life. And by contrast, it defined the middle-class, adult world of manicured lawns in the suburbs as "square." It drew a line that would later be redrawn by the Beatles and later again by L. L. Cool J and other rappers.

Elvis Presley was first recorded in 1954 by Sam Phillips, owner of a small independent record company in Memphis, Tennessee. On a quest to find a white male singer who could belt out R & B, Phillips discovered and signed not only Presley but also Johnny Cash, Carl Perkins, and Jerry Lee Lewis. Many people think that Presley recorded his best songs with Phillips, but he didn't become a national star until Victor bought his contract for forty thousand dollars in 1955. With hits such as "Heartbreak Hotel," "Don't Be Cruel," "All Shook Up," and "Treat Me Nice," Presley parlayed his brand of rock 'n' roll into thirty-eight gold records and sales of more than one hundred million platters by 1961. But as Presley became a business — a very big business — he lost touch with the blues, gospel, and rockabilly of his roots. Although his popularity continued to grow, Presley grew increasingly dependent on prescription drugs as he became more a crooner than a rocker, and his music became Las Vegas-style glitter pop.

African-American Rockers

Although born out of the African-American music of rhythm and blues, post-Elvis rock 'n' roll was dominated by white stars. But at the same time that Rosa Parks refused to give up her seat on that bus in Montgomery, several mid-1950s Black rockers refused to surrender their legacy and rose to the top of the field by the pure force of their talent and rock 'n' roll artistry.

With his raspy voice and the way he hammered the piano keys, Antoine "Fats" Domino remained true to pure rhythm and blues more than any other rock star. Born in New Orleans, he began recording at the age of twenty in 1948. In all, he sold over sixty million platters, more than anyone else in the 1950s except Elvis and Pat Boone. Sixty-five Fats Domino singles made the pop charts, including twenty-two gold records. His best known hits include "Blueberry Hill," "Blue Monday," and "Walkin' to New Orleans."

Although his popular success was short-lived in the 1950s, rock guitarist Bo Diddley went on to influence the playing styles of Buddy Holly, Muddy Waters, and later Bruce Springsteen. Born Ellas Bates in 1928 Mississippi and nicknamed after a mean fighting slave from southern folklore, Diddley earned his living as a street musician. His trademark was his rectangular guitar, and his best-known hits were "Bo Diddley" and "I'm a Man."

"Little Richard" Penniman came up in music as a gospel singer, and he used that gospel frenzy in his rock 'n' roll singing style. He began recording jump blues and R & B at sixteen in 1951, but he matured with his own style of raucous piano rock in 1955. "Tutti-Frutti," "Slippin' and Slidin'," and "Lucille" are among his many rock 'n' roll classics.

Above: The music of rock 'n' roll pioneer Chuck Berry has influenced everyone from the Beatles to the Beach Boys to L. L. Cool J.

Opposite: All shook up. Elvis Presley (top) gave rock 'n' roll an attitude of youthful rebellion and sexual energy. And while most rock 'n' rollers picked guitar, a few played piano, none more effectively than Fats Domino (bottom).

Played His Guitar Just Like A-Ringing the Bell

Even more than Elvis Presley, Chuck Berry succeeded in weaving Black and white musical traditions together in his rock 'n' roll. Trained as a blues musician, Berry was the first African-American to compose in the rockabilly style. And although Elvis Presley has the title "King of Rock 'n' Roll," based on pure musical talent, most people today would crown Chuck Berry as the Master.

Though he was thirty in 1956, Berry wrote and recorded songs that defined the spirit and concerns of America's teens, Black and white. He had a knack for witty lyrics packed with images of cars, school life, teenage girls, and rock 'n' roll itself. And when he sang, accompanied by the rapid fire of his guitar, he spit out the words with a crisp clarity uncharacteristic of blues singers. In live performances Berry set new standards for rock 'n' roll showmanship. He'd play his guitar behind his back, on his knees, while hopping across the stage on one foot, or while doing his trademark duckwalk. Even today, at around the age of seventy, Berry can still put on quite a show. But from 1955 to 1959, he electrified millions of U.S. teens with his stage shows and jumping hit songs, including "Maybellene," "Roll Over, Beethoven," "Johnny B. Goode," "Rock 'n' Roll Music," and "Sweet Little Sixteen." In the process, however, he became the target of the unofficial anti-rock campaign waged by some narrow-minded politicians. In a controversial trial, Berry was convicted in 1960 of a federal offense of driving an underage girl across state lines for immoral purposes.

American Bandstand, Payola, and Top-Forty Rock

By the end of the decade, Chuck Berry was on his way to jail, Elvis was in the army, Buddy Holly and Ritchie Valens were dead, Little Richard had found religion and renounced rock, and Jerry Lee Lewis had scandalized his public when he married his thirteen-year-old cousin. Rock 'n' roll, ruled by the fresh-scrubbed likes of Fabian, Paul Anka, and Bobby Rydell, hardly looked as

Please Mr. Postman

In 1993, the U. S. Postal Service released a set of seven stamps honoring pioneers of rock 'n' roll and rhythm and blues. Featured on the stamps are rockabilly original Bill Haley; Elvis Presley and early followers Buddy Holly and Ritchie Valens; R & B vocalist Dinah Washington; the great doo-wop harmonizer Clyde McPhatter; and soul singer Otis Redding.

though it was here to stay. The music took a sharp turn away from the African-American blues that had inspired it and concentrated on the wholesome gleam of its image. Settling into a commercialized cartoon of itself, rock 'n' roll was fronted by white teenagers whose musical talents were substantially below the likes of Chuck Berry, Fats Domino, and LaVern Baker.

The reasons for this development in rock 'n' roll were more political than artistic. In the guise of an investigation to clean up corruption in the music business, opponents of rock 'n' roll launched congressional investigations into a practice known as payola. Payola was a system in which record producers would bribe disc jockeys to play and promote their records. This practice was widespread, and such payoffs were common going back to the pluggers of Tin Pan Alley. But this investigation — and the criminal charges that came out of it — focused solely on rock 'n' roll. Even more selectively, the investigators harassed Alan Freed but spared Dick Clark. Freed championed rhythm and blues artists, denounced cover singers like Pat Boone, and openly struck back at rock 'n' roll's opponents. Dick Clark, whose daily after-school television show, "American Bandstand," was watched by twenty million teens from coast to coast, owned a big chunk of many of the records he played on the show. But because he promoted "wholesome" rock and "wholesome" teens, which usually meant no rebellious-looking guests, no R & B, and virtually no African-Americans, Clark was spared. Alan Freed's career was ruined, and in the late fifties and early sixties, Dick Clark's watered-down brand took over rock 'n' roll. But help was on the way.

With hard-rocking rhythms, clever lyrics, and innovative chord changes, the Beatles snapped American rock out of its early sixties slump.

The British Invasion

In the early 1960s, Donna Reed's TV daughter, Shelley Fabares, scored a big hit with "Johnny Angel," while African-American bluesmen Bill Bill Broonzy and Howlin' Wolf and rockers Chuck Berry and Bo Diddley had more fans in Britain than they had in the United States. When, in 1964, the Beatles, the Rolling Stones, and other British rock groups became sensations in the U.S., American rock rediscovered its roots.

The Beatles took their name from Buddy Holly's group, the Crickets, and many of their early recordings are updates of R & B and rockabilly. They did covers of Chuck Berry's "Roll Over, Beethoven" and Little Richard's "Long Tall Sally." And in "She Loves You," "Ticket to Ride," "Help," and many other John Lennon-Paul McCartney originals, sharp, witty lyrics combined with a bluesy rock beat to make original music with traditional roots.

The Rolling Stones, who took their name from a Muddy Waters song, were even more influenced by African-American R & B. Their debt to the blues can be seen in their recording of "Little Red Rooster" and covers of other Blind Willie Dixon songs, as well as in such Mick Jagger-Keith Richards originals as "Satisfaction" and "Jumpin' Jack Flash." Along with the Who, the Animals, and later Jethro Tull and Elton John, the Beatles and the Rolling Stones led a wave of British musicians in revitalizing rock 'n' roll in the States.

The Doors, Jefferson Airplane, the Grateful Dead, and the Byrds were among the more original and successful American rock groups. Although they re-established rhythm and blues in American rock, like the Beatles they continued to evolve and change. Musicians sometimes experimented with sitars and Asian music, and songwriters often tried out lyrics dense with poetic imagery and social messages.

Above: It took British groups such as the Rolling Stones to bring rhythm and blues back to American rock 'n' roll in the mid-1960s.

Below: Along with Ray Charles, Jackie Wilson (shown performing "Lonely Teardrops") set the standard for the African-American style of soul in the 1960s.

Soul

Although the British Invasion gave American rock a much needed shot in the arm by bringing rhythm and blues back home, African-American musicians had other ideas. Respectful as they were of the achievements of their predecessors, they were less interested in repeating the past than in moving on to new sounds. The most important of these new sounds was called soul.

Nearly every soul singer from Ray Charles and Jackie Wilson to James Brown and Aretha Franklin had early experience singing gospel, and the essence of soul is the runaway emotion of gospel. Soul singers were more influenced by Mahalia Jackson than by Fats Domino. Against a background of civil rights marches, dashikis, Afro hairstyles, and intense Black pride, soul was a music of ecstasy that celebrated African-American life with more joy than any music before or since. And like gospel, soul preached a message of love, even if the passion was more physical than spiritual.

Early masters of soul were Ray Charles and Jackie Wilson. With "What'd I Say," Charles set the model for setting lyrics about romantic love to the music of gospel, complete with a

"R-E-S-P-E-C-T." Soul music, as performed by Aretha Franklin, is a joyous expression of Black pride.

preacher-congregation call and response. Wilson, whose voice had an almost operatic range, put the scream in soul and the athletics into the soul stage act. His big hits were "Lonely Teardrops" and "Higher and Higher." During a typical jumping, screaming performance in 1975, Wilson suffered a heart attack and slipped into a coma from which he never recovered. Other masters of the soul style were Otis Redding, Sam Cooke, Wilson Pickett, and the integrated group from Memphis, Booker T. and the MGs.

Respect and Pride

But no one sang soul better than James Brown and Aretha Franklin, and perhaps no songs express the spirit of soul better than Brown's "Say It Loud — I'm Black and I'm Proud" and Franklin's recording of the Otis Redding tune, "Respect."

Born into poverty in rural South Carolina in 1934, Brown spent much of his childhood hustling dimes by racking pool balls, shining shoes, and tap dancing in the streets. He organized his first combo in prison while serving time for auto theft. Released early, Brown gave a sign of things to come in 1956 with his record "Please, Please, Please," two minutes and forty seconds of one word, "please," howled, squealed, panted, and screamed in gospel frenzy. Even more than Jackie Wilson, James Brown gave an electrifying stage show that earned him the nickname "the hardest-working man in show business." As he performed his songs he would jump, spin, fall, do splits, and finally collapse in a wild choreography of acrobatics. Then, as he was led off stage draped in a cloak by an assistant, he would throw off the cloak and fly into yet another rage of song and dance. His best hits, including "I Feel Good," "Papa's Got a Brand New Bag," and "Say It Loud," can be described as nothing less than bone rattling. Although his career nosedived in the 1970s and he was once again imprisoned, this time for drugs, James Brown's legacy has lived on in such varied performers as Mick Jagger, the Clash, Michael Jackson, and Hammer.

The Jackson Five (that's Michael, center) were among the many Motown chart-toppers of the 1960s and 1970s.

When Aretha Franklin sang "Respect," the song spoke not only for African-Americans in their fight against racism, but also for women, white and Black, in their struggle for equal opportunity. The daughter of a minister, Franklin began singing professionally at the age of fourteen. She sang with Mahalia Jackson, Sam Cooke, and the best gospel groups of the day. Foolishly, however, her first record company wouldn't let her make soul platters. But once she signed with Atlantic in 1967, she saw thirty-five of her records make the charts in the next seven years, including "A Natural Woman," "Chain of Fools," and "Think," each one delivered with the passion of a fiery sermon and sung, sometimes shrieked, with exquisite emotion.

Motown and Packaged Soul

Started in 1962, Motown became not only the first successful Black-owned record company, but by 1980 the largest Black-owned company in the nation. Motown founder and czar Berry Gordy, Jr., rose from his job as a Ford assembly-line worker to sign and produce many of the most successful African-American music acts of the 1960s and 1970s, including the Supremes, the Temptations, and the Jackson Five. But critics of the Motown sound charge that Berry did to soul what Dick Clark did to rock 'n' roll: he polished it but took out the punch.

The music of James Brown and Aretha Franklin was too wild and spontaneous, too outspoken and angry for Motown. Under Berry's coaching, Motown acts were guided to cut records with catchy love lyrics and a danceable beat. Berry brought string musicians from the Detroit Symphony Orchestra into the studio to give the Motown sound a refined finish. He also costumed his acts in formal wear and gowns, and the women wore piled-high bouffant wigs. To record for Motown in the 1960s, the talent had to attend classes on table manners and how to carry on small talk so they could move comfortably in polite society.

In an age of civil rights activism and the rise of the Black Panthers, Motown performers were contractually forbidden to make political statements, and the Motown sound and image were carefully designed to be non-threatening to white, middle-class Americans. As a result, from Smokey Robinson and the Miracles to Stevie Wonder, the Motown version of pop soul appealed to white record buyers more than any previous African-American music. It paved the way for the Rascals (Felix Cavaliere and other former members of Joey Dee and the Starliters) to lead several white groups in successfully recording some very soulful music, such as the Rascals' own "Good Lovin'."

The Many Faces of Rock Since the 1970s

The 1970s began with the breakup of the Beatles and the deaths of rock 'n' roll greats Jimi Hendrix, Janis Joplin, and Jim Morrison of the Doors. Left without clear artistic leadership, rock music splintered into dozens of substyles. The soft, introspective rock of singer-songwriters such as James Taylor and Carole King and the art rock of Emerson, Lake, and Palmer. The heavy metal perfected by Led Zeppelin and Aerosmith and the glamour rock of Queen and David Bowie. The southern rock of the Allman Brothers and pop R & B

The jukebox at the Supai Cafe

Supai is a town at the bottom of the Grand Canyon and home to four hundred Havasupai Indians. In the town cafe and in the huts throughout the primitive village, picture posters of Bob Marley adorn the walls, and reggae music can often be heard playing. No one knows exactly how or when reggae music was introduced to the Havasupai, who live in relative isolation from the rest of America. But we do know that the people embraced not only the reggae rhythms and beat, but also the Rastafarian religious vision expressed in Marley's music.

When American rockers such as War and Blondie imported the reggae sound into their records, they left behind the messages of African liberation from exploitation and of Jah, the Rastafari god of love, messages the Havasupai understoods. When Bob Marley died of cancer at the age of thirty-six in 1981, the people of Supai mourned for two weeks.

Freddie Mercury, lead singer for Queen and the first rock superstar to die of complications from AIDS.

of Diana Ross and Whitney Houston, Lionel Richie, and Luther Vandross. Each had its loyal fans, and each made millions. Within twenty years after it began as the music of teenage rebellion, rock became so popular and mainstream that it looked a lot like the white line in the middle of the road.

There were also counterstyles. Patti Smith, the Ramones, and the Sex Pistols spearheaded a music of anger and discord known as punk rock. Joan Jett, Pat Benatar, and Bruce Springsteen returned to fundamental rock 'n' roll. Paul Simon, Sting, Eric Clapton and many others experimented with the reggae music of Jamaicans Bob Marley and Peter Tosh. And more recently, alternative rock groups like Jane's Addiction and grunge rockers such as Nirvana have rebelled against slick, high-tech video rock. But the most important styles since 1970 have been disco, funk, hard rock, and rap.

Above: Disco didn't catch on in the U.S. until Donna Summer took her musical ideas to Germany, where she found sympathetic record producers.

Below: The stadium scoreboard meekly asks unruly fans to "Please Return to Your Seats" during an anti-disco promotion that got out of hand at a Chicago White Sox game.

Disco and Funk

Few musical styles have met with as much hostility as disco. In 1979, a Chicago disc jocky blew up ten thousand disco records between games of a White Sox doubleheader, inflaming thousands of anti-disco fanatics in attendance to riot. They had to cancel the nightcap. Indeed, the worst disco was machine-made dance music deserving of scorn. But the best was musically innovative.

Disco started in 1975, when Donna Summer, an African-American singer and songwriter from Boston, recorded "Love to Love You Baby." Produced in Germany, the song was seventeen minutes long, and the basic rock combo gave way to a combination chamber orchestra and swing band souped up with amplifiers and electronic gimmickry. Although Summer went on to be crowned the queen of disco, the Trammps were probably the most accomplished disco musicians. A twelve-piece ensemble with conga drums, tambourines, keyboards, guitars, and bass, the Trammps brought Latin American rhythms back to dance music.

Although such disco-adaptable dances as the Hustle came out of the African-American ghetto, disco soon became a white, middle-class craze. The 1977 movie *Saturday Night Fever* did for disco what *The Blackboard Jungle* did for rock 'n' roll twenty-two years earlier. It starred a working-class Italian-American disco dancer (John Travolta) and turned the Bee Gees into the first white disco superstars with their hit "Stayin' Alive." Other notable disco groups include A Taste of Honey, which featured two women lead vocalists, and the Village People, an integrated group that used theatrical costumes and campy humor in a stage show that appealed to gay and straight crowds alike. Though disco was virtually dead by 1980, some of the disco-bashing that killed it was based less on musical objections than on racism and anti-gay sentiments.

Reacting against disco and the pop soul of Motown was the African-American music called funk. Funk fuses soul with hard rock. As pioneered by the Chambers Brothers and Sly and the Family Stone in the late 1960s, funk rejected the studio polish and reliance on technology of the Motown sound and embraced instead the smear and smell of rhythm and blues. Nor did funk avoid controversial lyrics. In 1968's "Everyday People," Sly Stone boldly declared "we got to live together," calling for integration at the very height of racial tensions. Later, in the 1970s, he just as boldly used his immense musical talents to sing songs preaching Black nationalism.

Sly (Sylvester Stone, second from left) and the Family Stone, the models for George Clinton and funk.

Although funk never enjoyed the popularity of disco, it attracted some daring musicians. In the groups Parliament and Funkadelic, George Clinton used funk music as the basis for an African-American counterculture, rich with hip slang, outrageous costumes, and a philosophy of world peace. Even Motown got in on the act when the Temptations cut "Papa Was a Rolling Stone," one of their more unusual songs. Rick James defined funk for the eighties with hits such as "Superfreak." And Prince combined the flamboyant styles of Jimi Hendrix's guitar and James Brown's dancing into a masterful 1990s version of funk.

Jimi Hendrix and Hard Rock

Until his show-stealing performance at the Monterrey Pop Festival in 1967, Jimi Hendrix was better known in Europe than in the U.S. He had played with Joey Dee and the Starliters ("Peppermint Twist"), and his best shot at making money came as a warm-up act for the Monkees, a group of actors with varied musical talents. But almost every hard rock and heavy metal guitarist since 1970 has tried to fathom and copy the guitar technique of Jimi Hendrix. Hendrix played the

guitar as intensely as James Brown sang. Although songs such as "Hey Joe" show how deeply rooted to traditional blues his music could be, Hendrix is best remembered as an innovator. Inventing new uses for amplification and distortion, Hendrix plucked guitar licks like nothing ever heard before. Tragically, Hendrix died of a drug overdose in 1970. Although his legacy lives on in Led Zeppelin, Guns n' Roses, Aerosmith, and in much of the highly amplified, angry music of the 1980s and 1990s, most rock critics agree that none has yet recaptured the genius of the man who wrote "Purple Haze."

There has never been a more innovative and daring guitarist than Jimi Hendrix.

Glamorous R & B balladeer Whitney Houston, winning another of her record number of music awards.

The hope and grit of contemporary African-American life are captured in the raps of Queen Latifah and L. L. Cool J.

Breakers, Rappers, Scratchers, and Burners
(Dancers, Singers, Deejays, and Graffiti Artists)

MTV. Shiny CDs. The presidencies of Reagan and Bush. A twelve-year span when homelessness, AIDS, and violence rose to epidemic proportions, and civil-rights leaders screamed bloody murder as many gains spearheaded by Martin Luther King, Jr., were erased. White and Black America became dangerously separated. For example, while violent crime rates went down in 95 percent of U.S. neighborhoods, they skyrocketed in inner-city neighborhoods, particularly among the youth for whom gang culture became an almost irresistible way of survival in the face of economic hopelessness. By the mid-1990s, American kids, mostly Black, were dying from gunshots on city streets faster than American GIs were dying during the Vietnam War. Every two hours — bang — another youth or teen shot dead; a classroomful every two days.

In this environment, rap music rose from an urban folk music in the late 1970s to one of the most commercially successful and highly controversial styles of contemporary rock in the 1990s. While Whitney Houston was scoring big with seven straight number-one singles and Michael Jackson stylized gang violence in his "Beat It" video, rappers established themselves as the journalists of youth culture in the inner cities. Descended from a tradition of exaggerated boasting known in the ghetto as "the dozens," rap music arose in the mid-1970s. And together with break dancing and spray-paint graffiti, it became the outward characteristics of the Black/Hispanic youth subculture, hip-hop. In the Bronx, Joseph Saddler, who would soon gain national fame as Grandmaster Flash, perfected the basic techniques of rap by using two turntables to play two records at once, then switching the feed from one to the other into a single set of speakers to create an exciting mix of sound. Over these tracks, in a rhythmic shout style, Saddler and his brothers would chant rhymed narratives filled with rapid-fire images of ghetto life. This was music that suddenly made rhythm and blues and soul seem old-fashioned. The new realities of inner city life are chillingly captured in "The Message," a groundbreaking hit for Grandmaster Flash and His Furious Five.

Throughout the 1980s and 1990s, rap has continued to develop and reach a larger and more integrated audience. Since "I Can't Live Without My Radio" in 1985, L. L. Cool J has never been satisfied with repeating himself. He cut one of the first rap love songs ("I Need Love"), fused rap to original rock 'n' roll by sampling Chuck Berry riffs into "Go Cut Creator Go," combined reggae with rap, and was the first rapper to appear on MTV's "Unplugged." His artistic versatility is at its best in "Crossroads," where he incorporates a full orchestra to accompany the inventive wordplay of his rap, which gives a guided tour of the ghetto without glorifying violence. Run-D.M.C. helped to popularize rap with white listeners by collaborating with the heavy metal group Aerosmith on "Walk This Way." Hammer opened even more doors when he used the techniques of rap as the basis for more conventional songs showcased in his lavish stage productions. Queen Latifah and M. C. Lyte have emerged as the leading voices of women rappers, Arrested Development blends blues, folk, and even African beat into its raps, Digable Planets have turned more than a few heads by merging the traditions of jazz and hip-hop, and, led by the Beastie Boys and the Irish group House of Pain, more than a few white rappers have shown that they can master the style.

Sistah Souljah, a hardcore "gangsta" rapper whose controversial lyrics were singled out for criticism by candidate Bill Clinton in the 1992 presidential election. Criticism of rap has crossed lines of race, age, and gender. It has also raised the issues of censorship and freedom of speech — both subjects that have long yapped at the heels of R & B and rock 'n' roll.

The "G" Thang

As rap has become more flexible and diverse, one group of rappers has stayed firmly rooted to the violence of inner-city gang life. To the outrage and astonishment of many, "gangsta rap" has been featured in videos and achieved commercial success without compromising its lyrics and brutal edge. Arising from the gang-run neighborhoods of Los Angeles, gangsta rap uses a hard, unadorned beat and rampant profanity to tell stories of gangbangers, drug dealers, hookers, and hustlers who smoke "blunts" and pack "glocks." Gangsta rap first received national attention in the late 1980s when the L.A. group Niggaz Wit Attitude (NWA) released "Straight Outta Compton," a song about a Black policeman who harasses a Black youth to impress his white partner, and which urges inner city youth to take revenge. NWA broke up, but all of its members, Ice T, Dr. Dre, and Easy-E — joined by Sistah Souljah, the all-female group Boss, Latinos Cypress Hill, and Snoop Doggy Dogg — have gone on to become leading gangsta rappers of the 1990s.

But it has not been without backlash. Black and non-Black, male and female, young, old, and in-between, critics of gangsta rap object to the way it glorifies violence and drug use, to its almost clichéd use of obscenities, and most of all to its hatred of women as expressed in such songs as "Bitch Better Have My Money." Many radio stations have banned or censored rap lyrics that are sexually explicit or encourage violence, and rap music comes under daily attack from church pulpits and political grandstands. But defenders of the music point out that the blues, now accepted as a rich source of American heritage, were once attacked on similar grounds, and that the best raps can give us a view of inner-city reality that we will not get anywhere else. It's not pretty, but it's true, and for the rappers, it's an act of survival.

From rhythm and blues to rap, rock 'n' roll now spans over forty years. It is not only a history of our music, but also a model of how many of our cultures — African-American, Anglo-American, and Latino, male and female — and their musical traditions interact. In the worst of times, they will steal from one another, without giving credit or thanks until many years later. At other times, they will clash, each feeling superior to and disrespectful of the other. But in the best of times they coexist, each thriving, growing, and developing independently, ready for the rare but magic moments when they will combine with other heritages to make something new, exciting, and American.

1500	Three million American Indians live in several hundred tribal communities throughout North America, each with its own ceremonial songs
1600	Conquistadors introduce Spanish music to the Indian peoples of America
1755	British soldiers force mass deportation of thousands of French-Canadians from Acadia; many resettle in Louisiana, bringing Cajun music and culture with them
1817	Slaves in New Orleans are granted the right to sing, dance, and play music on Sunday afternoons in Congo Square
1843	The first minstrel show, the Virginia Minstrels, debuts
1863	The Emancipation Proclamation declares freedom for all slaves in states at war with the U.S.; music of the plantation will one day enchant post-Civil War America
1890	U. S. troops massacre three hundred Sioux Indians for singing and dancing in the Ghost Dance ceremony
1900	First hit records: whistling and laughing "coon songs" of ex-slave George Washington Johnson
1915-40	More than one million African-Americans leave their homes in southern states to relocate in the North and West, bringing blues, spirituals, and other music with them
1917	First jazz record issued (the Original Dixieland Jass Band playing "Livery Stable Blues" and "Tiger Rag" on the Victor label)
1920	Mamie Smith records the first blues record, "Crazy Blues"; it sells over one hundred thousand copies at nearly one dollar apiece; KDKA in Pittsburgh goes on the air, the first radio station with scheduled programs
1924	Louis Armstrong and His Hot Five help Chicago succeed New Orleans as jazz capital of the world
1927	Al Jolson sings "My Mammy" in Hollywood's first talking picture, *The Jazz Singer;* Duke Ellington and his orchestra open at the Cotton Club in Harlem; the country music industry begins when Jimmie Rodgers and the Carter Family record their hillbilly songs in Tennessee
1932	Blues pianist "Georgia Tom" Dorsey devotes himself to God's music and becomes the founding father of modern gospel
1936	Swing becomes America's music of choice as Benny Goodman and his Orchestra burn down the house at the Paramount Theater in New York City
1939	Americans across the the country drop millions of nickels in the 250,000 jukeboxes in service
1945	Bebop jazz launched as Dizzy Gillespie and Charlie "Bird" Parker record "Koko"
1950	Chicago, with the second-largest African-American population in the U.S., becomes the blues capital of the world
1952	The Moondog Coronation Ball in Cleveland, Ohio, opens the age of rock 'n' roll
1959	The Newport Folk Festival begins
1964	Louisiana fiddler Dewey Balfa performs at the Newport Folk Festival and sparks a revival in Cajun music; British invasion in full swing as the Beatles arrive for first U.S. tour
1965	Bob Dylan abandons his acoustic guitar for an electric to create folk-rock
1969	Guitarist Jimi Hendrix performs acid-rock version of the "Star-Spangled Banner" before crowd of five hundred thousand at the Woodstock Music Festival, ushering in new era of American music

1974	Bob Marley brings international attention to reggae music with his hit album *Natty Dread*
1981	MTV begins broadcasting, and music videos change the way pop music is marketed
1985	Conducted by Quincy Jones, forty-six rock and pop musicians collaborate to record Michael Jackson's "We Are the World" to benefit hunger-relief efforts in Africa
1991	2 Live Crew and other "gangsta" rappers come under attack for lyrics that allegedly promote racial and sexual violence; Lollapalooza traveling alternative music festival becomes an annual event

GLOSSARY

bebop
a highly improvisational style of jazz pioneered by Charlie "Bird" Parker and others shortly after World War II; features long solos and is played by small combos

blackface
the practice of late nineteenth- and early twentieth-century singers of blackening their face with burnt cork to exaggerate the appearance and mannerisms of African-Americans

blues
music derived from African-American folk songs about the difficulties and joys of surviving in post-Civil War America

cadenza
a flourish of notes, usually played by a horn on a solo jazz break; many musicians, such as Louis Armstrong, became famous for their signature cadenzas

cakewalk
from the minstrel shows, a showy strut around the stage, accompanied by music, usually performed by the entire company in the finale

call and response
the basic musical pattern of jazz and much American music; the lead instrument or singer plays a few notes and the rest of the ensemble or the chorus responds (Heidy-heidy-heidy-heidy? Heidy-heidy-heidy-ho!)

calypso
Caribbean folk music made popular in the U.S. by Harry Belafonte and others in the 1950s

coon songs
popular turn-of-the-century ballads portraying African-Americans in stereotyped situations

corrido
Mexican folk ballad that records the exploits of a folk hero

cover
the practice, common in the early days of rock 'n' roll, of recording a song previously recorded by someone else, often without giving proper recognition

cross-over
ability of a song or musician to appeal to both an ethnic audience and the mainstream

doo-wop
a style of rhythm and blues that relies on smooth vocal harmonies more than instrumentation

field holler
musical chants sung by plantation slaves; the forerunner of the blues

funk
a style of music that combines soul with hard rock and became an expression of the African-American counterculture of the 1970s

"gangsta" rap
controversial and often obscene music of the 1990s that expresses the details and desperation of contemporary gang life

Great Migration
the resettling, from the 1920s through the 1950s, of millions of African-Americans from the rural South to the urban North, bringing with them the blues, gospel, and other musical influences

Harlem Renaissance
centered in New York City of the 1920s and 1930s, a burst of African-American creative activity; found its musical expression in works of Duke Ellington, Eubie Blake, and others

hip-hop
African-American youth culture of the 1980s and 1990s characterized by rap music

jazz	characterized by improvisation and initially developed mostly by Black Creoles, a uniquely American music that sprang from the many musical influences present in late nineteenth-century New Orleans.
klezma	immigrant Jewish band music that combined folk and dance rhythms of Eastern Europe with the syncopation of American jazz
olio	opening act of traditional minstrel show, featuring a medley of songs, dances, and jokes
powwow	a gathering of American Indians to dance, chant, and preserve traditional customs
R & B	rhythm and blues; originally a term for any records marketed to African-American neighborhoods, R&B is more properly the combo dance music that bridged the gap between big band jazz and rock 'n' roll
shouts	African-American style of singing that began with the field hollers of the plantation and continued through blues and even into rap, when microphones and amplifiers made the shout style no longer necessary
ska	style of music combining the Caribbean rhythms of reggae with the instrumentation of jazz
stride	jazz piano style of the Harlem Renaissance popularized by Fats Waller
syncopation	the chief characteristic of ragtime, an intentional shift in the beat giving the music its jaunty sound
Tin Pan Alley	music publishing houses that employed hundreds of European immigrant songwriters and rose to the top of the American music industry in the first half of the twentieth century
world music	a movement of the 1980s and 1990s that promotes and borrows from the many folk musics of the world
zydeco	music of the Black Creoles of Louisiana, a distinctive folk music that uses cow bells and washboards as well as electric guitars to combine African and French-Canadian influences with rock 'n' roll

FURTHER READING

Ancona, George. *Powwow.* New York: Harcourt Brace Jovanovich, 1993.

Brown, Sandford. *Louis Armstrong.* New York: Franklin Watts, 1993.

Bufwack, Mary A. and Oermann, Robert K. *Finding Her Voice: Women in Country Music.* New York: Crown, 1993.

Cross, Brian. *It's Not About Salary: Rap, Race, and Resistance in Los Angeles.* New York: Verso/Routledge, 1993.

Finkelstein, Norman H. *Sounds in the Air: The Golden Age of Radio.* New York: Scribner, 1993.

Finn, Julio. *The Bluesman.* Brooklyn, New York: Interlink Books, 1992.

Haskins, James. *Black Music in America: A History Through Its People.* New York: Crowell Junior Books, 1987.

Hasse, John Edward. *Beyond Category: The Life and Genius of Duke Ellington.* New York: Simon and Schuster, 1993.

Heth, Charlotte, ed. *Native American Dance.* Washington, DC: Smithsonian Institution/Starwood, 1993.

Holland, Ted. *This Day in African-American Music.* Rohnert Park: Pomegranate, 1993.

Lantz, Fran. *Rock, Rap, and Rad: How to Be a Rock or Rap Star.* New York: Avon/Flare, 1993.

Wexler, Jerry. *Rhythm and the Blues.* New York: Knopf, 1993.

Wyman, Carolyn. *Ella Fitzgerald: Jazz Singer Supreme.* New York: Franklin Watts, 1993.

Laramie Junior High IMC

DATE DUE

OCT 2 0 1998		
MAR 0 8 1999		
JAN 2 3 2006		
APR 3 0 2008		
MAY 0 6 2008		